D0109898

Seeking
the
Wilderness

a Spiritual Journey

by Tim Lehman
Illustrations by Paula Diller Lehman

Faith and Life Press,
Newton, Kansas

Through the use of stories that narrate a Christian view of creation and the Bible, Seeking the Wilderness: A Spiritual Journey *invites readers to enter a spiritual walk with the earth.*

Printed on recycled paper in the United States of America

96 95 94 93 4 3 2 1

Library of Congress Number 93-71663
International Standard Book Number 0-87303-205-5

Editorial direction for Faith and Life Press by Susan E. Janzen; copyediting by Edna Krueger Dyck; design by John Hiebert; cover design by Gwen Stamm; cover photo ©1993 by Annie Griffiths/Westlight; printing by Mennonite Press.

I dedicate this book to my daughter, Kristin, for in her heart she holds the secrets of the future generation in love with life.

Table of Contents

Foreword

"In the beginning God created the heavens and the earth. And God saw that it was good." Seven times in the creation story it is repeated that God saw the creation as "good." God entrusted to humankind the care of the creation. Today we know that we have failed to fully care for the world and that such failure is sin in God's sight, to the detriment of humankind, all of the created world, and the Creator.

Tim Lehman shares with readers his wilderness hiking, camping, and canoeing experiences where he is immersed in experiencing creation with body, mind, and soul. The journeys have taken him far into God's will.

In these wilderness experiences all pretense is dropped as he grapples with the elements of God's creation and discovers a closer relationship with the Creator. He witnesses beauty in the sunset, hears the call of the loon, and finds a deepening relationship with his companions on the journey. He knows the struggles of keeping warm in the sudden summer hailstorm or the cold of winter's snow. He has known the near panic of losing his way. On his shoulders rests the weight of the safety and well-being of others on the journey.

This book is a journey with Tim into both physical and spiritual wilderness. It is the story of humankind struggling for existence in a physical world. But more than that, it is the story of humankind struggling to find God. And in the struggle it is not humankind who find God, but God who finds humankind.

In his perceptive way, Tim ably expresses his deepest responses to God. His gift for poetic, descriptive expression enables the reader to hear God's call in a like manner. Those who have been challenged by rugged hiking trails, those who have canoed rushing waters, or those who have stared into the stillness of a starlit sky will recall their experiences.

Those who have not had these experiences will relate their lifetime journey of meeting challenges, finding joy, and the satisfaction of overcoming obstacles as they traveled in God's company.

Think of a canoe trip as a mini slice of life. In this experience we face the simple dependence of coming face-to-face with God and walking with that Presence. So it is with life itself.

This book can be savored in many readings. It is not a Bible study guide, although Scripture references are frequent and are the basis of many of the meditations. Nor is it a study of creation theology. This is a devotional book that challenges us to examine our relationship with God as we walk with Tim on his journey.

It is a timely book that speaks to us today when we no longer are in close touch with the natural environment. Many do not raise their own food or do not breathe fresh air. We are never too hot or too cold. This separation has also tended to separate us from God, the Creator. Planned times in the out-of-doors, such as the wilderness experiences described here, serve to keep us in touch with creation and our Creator.

Finally, we are reminded of God's justice that will enable all to live in harmony on the earth. Living a life of justice enables humankind to be at one with God and all that God created in the heavens and the earth. May God grant us the vision and courage to follow the call to live justly in harmony with the Creator and the Created.

Jocele T. Meyer
Mennonite Central Committee Global Education
Member of Joint Environmental Task Force
of the Mennonite Church and
General Conference Mennonite Church

Author's Preface

Somewhere deep inside each of our hearts a kernel of truth lies in wait. Occasionally uprooted and uncovered by life's calamities and pleasures, we stumble onto it and recognize the beauty in its honest revelation. This book is less about a schema of propositions and more about a discovery of self. I have written the words in the chapters that follow because I have lived them. They now own a part of me that continues to develop.

For those of you who will read this book, I ask one thing. As you read, allow the uncovering of your own life's kernel. Let the stories and the musings engage you at a level where you really live. Do not accept these words as your words, but challenge them, reject them, and perhaps listen to them as you would hear the wind refresh the day or cool the night.

Any book that advertises a spiritual content can be of value only if it presents a risk to the writer and the reader. As we enter the following pages together, we form a partnership of rediscovery. The content of our faith waits for us, not just here, but in our growing awareness of God's presence within all of our world. This book proclaims such a presence.

My motive for writing is not persuasion. I don't intend to tell people how to feel or think or be. Rather, my motive is to share my personal experience and my personal faith. While this may sound strange or self-centered, I believe it to be the most honest way in which I can share myself in relationship. The gift I give is honesty, and it is engagement. To share it with you is one of my utmost pleasures.

I am aware that much of the content of *Seeking the Wilderness* does not conform to traditional Christian emphases. I am just as aware that traditional Christian teaching has not shared with us much of a positive bias for biblical insights into creation and our place in it. Therefore, we are left without guidance, without direction, and without an earthly mandate, for we do not often hear of creation's value.

At the same time, we witness the destruction of the earth, and we participate—though often reluctantly.

We find ourselves at a critical juncture. Much of life seems confusing and hollow. Do we save the whales or just save souls? Should we hug a tree of build another house? Do we sing the praises of a future world or strive to save the one God has already made? These questions seem endless and they seem to exist without answers that satisfy. Perhaps the questions themselves only serve to polarize the problem and preserve it. What if we did not ask such questions, but rather nurtured a relationship with the world about us as if it really were God's? If this book does anything, it shares the way in which one person seeks to nurture a relationship with God through the medium of the things God owns and loves and creates. I can say with all my heart that this world has been the stage where God has met me and changed me.

Is there yet hope that Christian people in general will embrace the world as if it were God's arena of incarnation? Can Christian people search beyond theological truisms for relevant and dynamic responses to the needs of our global environment? Is it too late to confront the Christian church with the challenge to engage and love the earth? This book speaks of a renewed hope that the time is right for broadening our theological horizons. Within the last decade, Christian writings on the environment have proliferated. Church people in many denominations and many locations are coming to the fore on behalf of the earth. Perhaps the time is just right to begin leading the church into a relationship of intimacy with God's creation. Could it be that we are ready to allow our relationship with this planet to mature and help shape the way we teach, preach, and read the Bible?

Finally this all funnels down into a focus on the nature of our spirituality. Is God's Spirit within us vibrant and engaged? Are we animated by the creations of God? Will we seek renewal in the places that we have not already claimed for our own?

Wilderness may depend on our careful stewardship for its survival, but wilderness does not reflect our image. Wilderness surely holds the power to infuse us with spiritual self-transcendence because we have done nothing to make it or enhance it or modify it. Wilderness therefore becomes a mighty symbol for God's good earth. Wilderness represents the possibility for humans to live in the simple harmony of God's covenant with creation. Wilderness illustrates a part of God's creation that has not seen the destructive hand of humanity. Wilderness can be a symbol for the reconciling of all relationships under the authority and intent of God, a biblical nirvana that calls to us with the sweet music of the soul.

Wilderness, as discovered and explored within the pages of this book, remains as much a part of the heart and soul as it does the natural environment. I invite you to enter this wilderness with me. Let us together look inward and outward for God's Spirit to guide us. The biblical theme of wilderness represents a person's need to be apart and be with God. The Bible stories about people of faith seeking God chronicle the dramatic effect of the wilderness experience. People of faith are changed into faithful people full of God's love and passion for life. Today, we may still seek God by seeking the wilderness.

Acknowledgements

It is with great pleasure that I give thanks to many people for their invaluable help in bringing this manuscript to its present form. I recognize my debt to my dear friends Perry Krehbiel, Jay Goering, and E. Fred Goering, who shared many lunchtime discussions with me, encouraged me, and read some of the early chapters. I thank all the summer staff persons from Wilderness Wind, who labored so energetically with me over the last seven summers. I especially thank Kathy Landis and Cheryl Mast, who have given so much of their time and energy to Wilderness Wind. I thank my friend and co-leader, Perry Yoder, from whom I have gained much insight into the wilderness of heart and woods, and I thank him for reading and commenting on the manuscript while it was still in rough form. I thank those persons who have served over the years on the Wilderness Wind board of directors, for they have always contributed to my dreams and vision. I must also thank the many, many persons who have traveled the northwoods under my leadership. They were wonderful, trusting souls, willing to brave many things with patience and joy. I especially thank Diane Zaerr for her friendship and encouragement as we tramped portage trails and canoed the lakes of the Quetico. I thank Susan Janzen, who has spent so many hours editing the manuscript and helping shape it into a more readable form. And I thank the staff of Mennonite Voluntary Service who shared the vision of the Creation Care Voluntary Service Unit, which allowed me much needed time to write. I thank those others who have read the manuscript with understanding and care: Jocele Meyer, Calvin DeWitt, Helmut Harder, Wes Jackson, Oswald Goering, and Grant Thompson. Your willingness to give time and thought to this work has been a real gift.

I also want to thank my family for their support of me and their role in shaping me over the many years of being together. My parents, Weldon and Vera Lehman, have probably done more than anyone to give me the necessary love which I have needed to mature emotionally and spiritually. Over the years my sisters and brother have stuck by me and loved me even though the miles are long between us. Most of all I want to express my appreciation for my wife, Paula, and my daughter, Kristin. Paula has been my constant mentor in almost every phase of this writing project. She has encouraged me over and over, she has corrected me, she has loved me through the long hours of writing. Kristin, too, has been more of a support than she probably knows. She has endured night after night as I headed off to the computer to work. She has been an inspiration to me through her natural love of the wilderness. I can think of no one with whom I would rather share the excitement and solitude of the wilderness.

Tim Lehman
January 1993

In the beginning, God.
  Created the heavens and the earth ...
    Proclaimed the light of day ...
      Proclaimed the dry ground ...
        Proclaimed the seas' gathering ...
  Proclaimed the greening of the earth ...
    Proclaimed the day and night ...
      Proclaimed the creatures of sea and air ...
  Proclaimed the creatures of the land ...
    Proclaimed humanity ...
  And it was good,
    AND it was good,
      And IT was good,
        And it WAS good,
          And it was GOOD,
          And it was good,
            AND IT WAS GOOD.
  In the beginning, God.

                    Genesis 1
                    author's paraphrase

Chapter 1

A Place of Belonging

Crab Lake

I am alone, yet surrounded and held close. A granite rock contours roughly to the shape of my back. Each point of quartz or nub of mineral indents my skin through the thin cotton shirt I wear. No, my back will not complain, for the rock, ageless as it seems, cradles into me the warmth gained from its exposure to the sun. Nighttime envelops me like a thick curtain of fog, while a distant moonlight filters and dodges through thin vapor clouds. My closest companions today, a chipmunk and black bear, have left me for places of better forage.

I am alone, yet feel no loneliness. Water moves toward me, reflecting glimmers of moonlight on its gentle curls. Each wave kisses this granite rock with a wet pat of tenderness. The rhythm lulls my thoughts into solitude. Behind me towers a forest of pine and birch. The trees have also grown into a comfortable existence on the lap of this expansive granite

1

rock. These dear friends of mine who silently guard my campsite are strong and brave. The trees blanket the world behind me as the water flows before me. I cannot imagine a place of more safety for my mind and my spirit. Soothed by the breeze off the lake, my senses ingest smells of damp wood and vegetation along the waters' edge, fresh pine odors from the forest, and the occasional wisp of campfire smoke.

Crying from somewhere on the lake, a loon cuts the silence with its sharp call. The invitation is repeated with an urgent pleading. Am I asked to join this skilled and gifted creature? The call wakens my mind to rhythms of time, unmeasured, except by annual migrations and cycles of life. This bird, this voice of night, collects romance and wonder in the pools of my timid spirit. In this place, with this call, I become enchanted with the challenge of wild places. And with each echoed cry I fall in love again with the spirit of this place.

The dark has fallen after the slow decline of light known to these long northern summer days. Sleep resists the temptation of a warm tent and keeps its distance because of my sense of rapture at a stillness I cannot understand. This stillness goes beyond comfort or enjoyment or even wonder. This stillness grips my soul with a locking iron bar of grace. Grace because I have contributed nothing to the joy I feel, nothing but the strength of paddling and portaging to get here. Grace because I am so small within the universe of created things; I actually feel my temporary existence. And why not? When I lounge atop what scientists call a four-and-a-half-billion-year-old rock, the thought of my lifespan passes through my mind quickly and is gone. All I think about is the continuance of grace radiating from this resting place.

Earlier today my water path connected with that of a female black bear swimming across a wide channel. This young bear was not impressed by my canoe or by my determination. But I was impressed by the big furry ears and shining black nose inching above the water as the lunging of huge padded feet propelled it swiftly to the far shore. Upon our chance meeting I knew that I had once more come to a world of life in unveiled form. Was I the visitor from another planet? Was I trespassing on God's garden of pleasure? I did not see signs to block my passage or any warnings of danger. No, I met the Gatekeeper of this ancient land, who graciously invited me to stay the night.

And what a night it has become. Silence lurks, even in the small night sounds that occasionally wake me from slumber. This silence wells up inside me even as it flows within the dark reaches of deep marsh-stained waters, or in the dark recesses of timber, or in the dark distances of space. Silence and darkness are welcome here tonight because I know they are much alike within the human mind. Both form frightening images to people who have not looked beyond the guarded boundaries of thinking. Yet both form places of renewal and imagination when fear is seen for the facade that it is. I think back to a poem written by Ulrich Schaffer: "The silence renews me as I sink into myself and lose the weight of worlds. . ." (*Searching for You*, Harper and Row, 1978). Silence is a friend I cherish. Tonight darkness allows me the peace to sink into silence with a detachment I have only known in a wild place. I lose myself in this dark silence. I am lost in an ocean of thoughtlessness buoyed by uncontrolled feelings that leave me on this rock while I transport myself into time, future and past. The rock is my anchor, the darkness my guide; the destination is endless. Darkness comforts, while lostness quiets fear, and I am relieved again from my compulsion to be in control.

I watch the stars. Stars have a magnetic quality on a wilderness night as they lift me out of gravity's hold. Each careful step on uncertain ground is lightened by their pull. I cannot feel my full weight as I sit or stand or lie here, because some distant galaxy draws my attention. Stars are   also alive in the way they show their light with stuttered intensity, as if to wink at me their pleasure. The beauty I see is in the grand scope of multitudes of dancing firelights that form shapes and patterns. Then, when I close my eyes, I see them again with even greater movement. And so I bask in my insignificance and laugh at being without control. I love grace.

Releasing control has taken real effort. I paddled down the north arm of Burntside Lake to avoid most of the summer cabins and motorboats. I worked in the face of wind and a light rain. A mile-long portage, carrying pack and canoe, added to the distance I have needed to be alone. Though not far from civilization's traffic, I have left it miles behind. This night the shores of Crab Lake will greet no other human warmth but mine. But through the many nights I have spent in different wilderness settings I have learned that even great physical effort will not guarantee the release for which I look. For if I can make it happen it remains within my control. My life is spent learning this lesson again and again.

The breath off the lake chills me, though I stubbornly resist movement. I want to hold onto the very moments that I know I do not hold. The cool air is chilling, but fresh with spirit. Where is its source? And where will it end? It too blows out of my control and so has power over me and refreshes me. The Spirit of God that hovers over the primordial waters of the world steals warmth from my bare arms and face as I lie here. Breath of God stirring the lake's surface and bending the leaf stems of birch trees, breathe into my memory so that I will not forget this place and this time. May the Gatekeeper always let me pass the entrance to your garden.

Before I give over to sleep, I have nothing to give back to the night but my gratitude—to say thank you for showing me the cradle of my belonging.

Morning light brings my mind slowly awake. The sleeping bag rustles as I move, and the jacket I folded last night still pillows my head. A slap of water just offshore tells me the fish already greet the day. Here inside this tent I am a caterpillar, having spun my web of nylon. But I will not emerge the butterfly, not with this sleep still in my eyes and face and hands. I slowly pull on wool pants and sweater to ease my body's adjustment to the cold morning air. I reach for my little treasures that give me confidence in this wild setting—lock-back knife, compass, and lighter. The tearing sound of the nylon zipper wakes me further as the tent door falls open to a new world. I cannot believe the transformation. Was last night only a dream? I feel torn away from my night of passion and my memory seems untrue. If I could go back to darkness as my nighttime blanket and stay within my comfortable rock cradle I would do so, for morning has brought me back to my timidity.

Painstakingly slowly, I crumble forward, out through the small cocoon doorway with complaints from all my body's joints. My feet feel swollen and tender. It takes all my effort to straighten up to my full height since my backbone seems cemented together in an unnatural shape. Even my woolies cannot keep away the chill of the morning as my skin tightens; my shivering is uncontrolled. I am awake now, but not pleased with the thought. Stumbling into the woods to relieve myself I take no notice of life around. Then kneeling beside the campfire I pull a large, flat rock away to discover a few burning embers still aglow. Yes, last night was real.

Finally, as the small campfire snaps and smokes its way past a pot of water, I open my eyes to the lake. A cauldron, a boiling sea could not produce more steamy mist. It is as if those vapor clouds from the night descended with a vengeance to suck life from their victim, the lake. The shroud of mist forms a fantasy world of shapes—zoo animals and prehistoric images. Uncontrollably, my excitement swells at the view as my sleep-logged body responds with new birth. I have canoed through mists like this as beads of moisture collected on my eyelids and dripped from my nose. I cannot help remembering the rise and fall of the canoe as we pushed through cloud banks that kissed the water and caressed every fiber of equipment and clothing. New worlds to explore was always the magnet that drew us through the mist.

But the only boiling now is in the coffee pot. A cup of coffee and a handful of oatmeal to throw into the remaining boiling water is a welcome breakfast, simple and substantial. Raisins, though not my choice of fruit, give me morning energy. Leaning against an old pine backrest and sipping a second cup of coffee, I can again study being alone. This is such a rare occurrence that I adjust to it clumsily. My life is filled to overflowing. I burst with plans laid upon plans and more plans. Why then does my heart always bring me back here to the woods and water? Why can my best laid and executed plans look bare against the blue sky breaking through the mist just now?

I am alone, yet I feel encircled by every sort of companion on this damp morning. Why does water speak to some and not to others? Why do trees whisper into one ear and not another? Why does solid, dead rock come alive in my presence? The answer is nothing that I can understand, but it is truth about my life. Whatever else is real about life and love and happiness, I know beyond a doubt that I belong to this place. I am owned by this world of matter and nothing belongs to me. Grace is being given a place to belong and knowing when you are there.

How can I have possibly found a place of belonging at the very time my life seems so insignificant? With all that has gone before me in this place and all that will follow, I get lost in the myriad expressions of life. Why should I be filled to overflowing with this crazy, nonsense of being in the only place where I can truly be owned, and held close, and loved? Have I filled the lake with my tears? Have I raised the trees with my fingers, pulling them skyward? Have I crushed and compressed these rocks into mortared cushions? Have I planned one event of my life to benefit the creation of my companions here? Either I must admit complete failure or complete dependency. In a life driven by my personal grasp of what is to be and what is not to be, here I must face mortality. Here I cannot turn from my weakness. It is here and now that I can touch and smell and breathe into myself blessings.

Blessings? I mean that which is given to me. No, not me alone, but to me as a human created by desire beyond any dream or thought's control. For that which I personally devise throughout my life cannot return to me as blessing, only as payment due. Blessing is something few human creatures learn to accept. If we are given a gift, we owe one in return. If we seek a favor, we must repay. We either move through life guilt ridden from our debts, or we think life owes us for all that we have done. Both positions lack the resources needed to receive blessing. Experiencing the blessings here at Crab Lake is all about seeing life from the perspective of the creature that I am. It is about finally acknowledging that I must receive from God my creator everything that makes life possible and celebrative. And when I am given the grace to see the reality of this blessing, I have found the longing of my heart—a lasting sense of belonging.

I stand to stretch and take a break from the coarse rock and tree bark. My movement reminds me that I am still here in body as well as in spirit. The sun has now fully burst over the forest with shoots of light that beam right through the mist above the lake. With this display, who can know whether today is the first or last day of creation? This day is so fresh that I soak it up like a dry sponge and feel as if I am swelling greatly with wet, new life.

My eyes catch a glint of sun off the bottom of my canoe. As I study the canoe's shape—as I often have—I feel satisfaction, knowing my hands made it, caressing the wood into its proper place. Its wooden gunnels lie against the grass and rock, sheltered among the trees. Its simple shape grows more elegant in these surroundings. I try to ignore the coating of clear fiberglass that seems less than a natural part of life here. The blending of shapes and textures and materials within this wilderness setting is worthy of much attention. Though the granite rock and the wood of the trees and the water all are such varying elements, here they are gently brought together. There is a community here that could teach all human endeavors how to exist in harmony. Paddling out from camp I expect sadness to follow me. But rather, I have a new canoe partner. This sense of belonging is a friend to be carried through life, not a temporary illusion.

The loon is back! Contesting my retreat he dives under my bow, only to emerge further ahead. His body drips with sparkling moisture over clear patterns of black and white. A muffled hoot escapes his throat seconds before he dives again from my sight!

My prayer is thanksgiving, for the Gatekeeper has allowed my exit. No toll is required for my newfound friend.

Distance Over Time

What have we inherited by way of our human story? A way of conflicting life within the world? Struggle for existence in a hostile country? Perhaps we face our time on this planet prepared to survive whatever the cost. One thing we can know for certain. Today we embrace a world that is no longer God's creation, for we have removed creation from our theology. We have done this with our power. We have, over time, limited and even denied any meaningful sense of

God's creative and sustaining investment within the lives of rocks, water, trees, air, and all the creatures that crawl, fly, swim, and run. No, I am not speaking only of rhetoric, but also of violent action. No, I am not meaning to affront the pious—only those whose piety forgets belonging. For there is no place for the Christian to belong but in the community of created things.

Harsh words perhaps, but justified as the human mammal continues its dominance. This is not a book on statistics and scientific research into the ecological crisis. Thankfully I acknowledge recent contributions from Christian brothers and sisters that clearly point to the ways humankind has laid so much of our planet to waste. From South American rain forests, to city smog, to oil spills, to nitrates in drinking water, to hazardous chemicals and nuclear wastes, to overfilled landfills, to ozone destruction, to depletion of aquifers, to acid rain, to the bombing ranges of U.S. military bases, to continued coal, silver, nickel, and gold mine tailings, to thousands of nonbiodegradable products mass produced and consumed on a daily basis, to industrial wastes in our rivers, to multiple hydroelectric dams warming and slowing our rivers, to loss of governmental protection of wild lands, to clear cut forests, to the rapid extinction of species—to all of the above and much more, the caring Christian enters into a holocaust sensation not unlike Revelation 8 and sounding of the seven trumpets.

We humans have not come this far toward separating our ties to the good earth without a long and painful process. No, this is not the time or place to put the blame on the industrial revolution or on certain technological advances, just as we must also not suggest that technology will someday save us from ourselves. The long and painful process of distancing from creation has been, and is first of all, a spiritual crisis, not economic or political or industrial. So let us stop pointing fingers and blaming an out-of-control secular process. For as long as we place blame outside ourselves, we—as good Christian caretakers—remain locked within an unchanging system. Placing blame accomplishes nothing but a temporary and false ease of conscience. And placing blame is a most basic form of denial.

Since history's beginning, humans have sought to control their world. We moderns are probably no more pathological on that score than early Mesopotamian civilization. The difference is that we now have far more sophisticated tools, as well as more people to wield them. Therefore, our spiritual distance from the earth, sky, and sea becomes more and more painful and destructive. Let us make no mistake as people who claim a Judeo-Christian allegiance to the biblical text. The only solution is spiritual. And the only place to begin is within ourselves. Our human story of painful distancing can only end as we open ourselves to belonging in a world we do not control, when we willingly give up dominance for participation, and self-love for coexistence within the loving arms of one creator God.

On an Island in Kawnipi

As the wind sifts through jack pine needles, it makes an almost hissing sound. Waves, power driven by the wind, slam against the bow of this island ship on Kawnipi Lake's great spreading body. Helpless, I study the endless parade of marching waves as they try to swallow the granite boulders piled along the shore. I feel fortunate to have made it to the protection of this island. This island itself is but an oversized boulder with grass and a few trees growing out of its cracks. But compared to Kawnipi's anger, the boulder looks pretty good.

Another solo canoe trip, this time into Canada's Quetico Provincial Park, and I am learning patience. With an entire afternoon ahead and miles to paddle, I simply sit cross-legged, squinting down the barrel of miles of water churned into three and a half foot waves. I can almost feel the roll of the boulder like a ship's hull searching for firm bottom. This afternoon caps four days to myself with six more to come. Sitting here watching the water dance, I begin to sense that my plight here on this island has little to do with the few hours I will lose on today's journey. Rather, it has everything to do with the frustration I experience in this interruption. What have I lost and what have I gained by my stay here?

I have been so careful to plan every detail of this trip and yet I have not allowed for interruptions. I have not allowed for the in-breaking of nature, thrusting upon me as sure and confident as an eagle's flight. If only the wind could be managed with calculations or machines—perhaps a dam across the sky.

Enough of this self-pity. Explorations on a wilderness island lure curiosity from these paddle-worn bones. I seek the protection of the southeast shore, away from the wind, and there find familiar bushes of sweet gale. This hardy shrub seems to withstand any punishment the elements can give. I, on the other hand, can certainly not boast the same. With great care I browse through these bushes for leaves and nutlets. Tea from the leaves and a sage-like spice from the nutlets provide the incentive. Suddenly I feel the pleasure of a gardener gathering the crop of beans or beets or cauliflower. If only I could discover a wild blue iris or the slender arched stem of a wild columbine jeweled with delicate beauty. These would not be gathered but enjoyed only for the view. The gardener and the artist in me relax. I study the shape and character of the rock deck of this island. Up close, very close, it is easy to see all the breaks in the rock's surface where various grasses and even wild blueberries take hold. Within the folds of ancient granite skin lie recesses dark and moist. No virgin soil here, for wind-borne seeds long ago sank roots stronger than granite into cracks deepened by their strength.

My island explorations have brought me home again and

I curl up gratefully amid the grass and cobbled surface of the rock. Will sleep come to me while the ocean seems to rage at my doorstep? Actually the raging seems less and a smooth rhythmic singing grows stronger in my mind. To sleep at home on a ship at sea or nestled on wilderness bedrock is amazing and draws me closer to the reality of why I have come here. Here dreaming answers my earlier frustration, for I have found a peaceful dream. In this dream I travel beyond myself and all my mental stations of security. Here resides no rational understanding of my well-being, but it is a surging, lifting buoyancy like riding the waves of my unconscious.

I awake and observe the irony of my peaceful sleep. Here where I thought I would cringe in regret for the wind, here God moved me into further crevasses of fertility. This place of all the stops I might have made has become Bethel, the gate of heaven. Ancient Jacob, you son and father of people like myself, let me walk with you on your journey to find God. Our journey begins here. God is where I rest peacefully and where I dream beyond myself. God is where I sleep on a bed fashioned and fixed to the very crust of the earth itself, where I become reattached to the very core of life within this planet.

I rise and move about the island once again. Grains of the rock have wedged their way into my pores. Mist off the waves flows into my lungs. Pine sap glues dark humus to my fingers while the smell of this place tickles my nostrils. I will drink tea raised by the sun and soil and water. There is not one part of my body that is not somehow connected to this place; my spirit gains shape by the very stuff of organic material. Could it be that God's almighty Spirit, which creates the earth, connects with my spirit through the medium of created matter? If so, then I have again found my place by God's side, in God's hand. I am on fire in a cradle of loving passion.

To belong here is so natural that words are wasted on the thought.

God Saw That It Was Good

"God saw that it was good." This sentence is repeated six times in Genesis 1 before there is any mention of the human creature. God is the actor, the arranger, indeed the creator. Everything that God brings into being is good. At the end of the sixth day the summary statement reads, "God saw all that was made, and it was very good."

This statement celebrates life. In its repetition it provides a unifying structure to the chapter. This indeed is the original "good news." That God creates everything good is a message that ought to restore faith and faithfulness. This "good news" is a call to worship, a call to hope in troubled times. To know that God is only about good things is to affirm each grain of sand and green leaf and wild animal call in the night.

Notice, if you will, that the only announcement of "good news" for the creation of humanity comes in verse 31 quoted above. It is most interesting that this statement only affirms humanity from within the context of all things created by God. My mind strains at the potential of this thought. What if humanity's context is indelibly linked to this affirmation of goodness? What if we are fundamentally created to exist within the natural? And what if our only hope for wholeness is from being rooted in and connected with each element and life form in creation?

Finally, what if a most basic experience of God comes through the natural processes and beauty of life? Some examples: the life and death and rebirth of wild fowers, the slow, ever-changing erosion of rocks and plains and mountaintops, the sucking of wolf pups in their den, the movement of water through a river course and through the tissues of our bodies. Or would you think the human being to be a freak of nature? Should we then strain for God beyond the limits of common things?

Finding God may not be as difficult as losing God. For it would seem by our actions that we humans have spent lifetimes getting away from a natural relationship with our Creator. Even today we manufacture every kind of machine that separates us further from our beginnings, from our genesis. We have objectified even the narrative of origin as if Genesis 1 is not really our story. But if not ours, then whose?

In this life we experience an incredible amount of sadness. This can be seen in our searching. We are a people cut off by our own cravings; we have misdirected them into ourselves. The more we seek life's meaning from human resources alone, the greater the distance we put between ourselves and everything else. What brings us wholeness? What satisfies? Is it a success measured by our possessions or is it in finding the connections and relationships God has placed in nature? Somehow human sadness is understandable from the way we have painted ourselves into a corner, separated from the doorway of nature. We are cut off. And if we are cut off from created things, then we are cut off from God.

You see, if Genesis 1 is our story, then human nature cannot be defined or even identified apart from our environment. There is no person aside from the person who lusts for the green of springtime, who laughs with the song of morning birds, who runs just to feel the wind and pound the earth. There is no person aside from the person who listens for the approach of a summer storm, who strives to find the movement of deer within the woods, who sorrows with the passing of all living things.

So as we separate from life forms around us, we let regions in our minds die. We close areas of emotion that need release as we further limit our contact with the wild. As the natural resources and habitats of this world diminish, so does our humanity. And because of this process of scaling down the human spirit, we have chosen to redefine ourselves. We call ourselves gods and go about drunk with ambition.

Everything becomes an object in our path. Even the narrative of our faith becomes a tool used to tear at the web of life. Instead of personally entering nature's doorway of Genesis 1 and becoming matter for God to mold, we choose to write our own creation story by our lives. Then of course we are left with the dilemma of the Bible itself, which to us has become a book of blasphemy. All-knowing gods that we are, we cleverly suck out its life and fashion it within our own lives, like wax museums on the move.

Yet one problem remains. We are empty or filled with turbid emotions covering our emptiness. Is there not one place where existence lies beyond our grasp, where hope still lingers on the lips of despair?

Broken Yokes

We are a tough-eyed crew coming off the portage trail at Canyon Falls. Weariness stains our determined features; smiles are scarce. Mud is a reality of life, especially from the knees down, with scattered patches on elbows and buttocks. Blood is present, too, but only occasionally showing.

The path dropped in elevation, though it fell only to rise again, over and over until the last descent. Winding through the ancient tree trunks and blundering along granite boulder fields, this guideline through the woods seemed a test of cruel fate. Once, when the trail suddenly dropped eight feet into a small ravine, I wondered if I would make it. Oh, I hate to slide a canoe off my shoulders when I know that I must heave it up again. Sledding the canoe down that drop, the rocks clawed with shrieking voices at the hull.

One canoe yoke broken, and a half day's travel ahead.

At least the rain no longer makes much of an impression, with all the sweat coming through our clothes. We find pleasure in knowing the trail has an end. Yet further into the day, each hour passing before our paddles, the rain's end will not be known. And so we camp a fourth night, determined to outlive this span of wet weather.

On our fifth day out we struggle to joke about the rain. We design a contest for estimating the time of sunshine's resurrection. It does not work and the rain continues, never stopping for very long.

By the eighth day, we take confidence from our survival and from the ugly condition of each others' appearance. We are together and even remembering the downpour of our second day out cannot separate us.

It had been late that second afternoon, with one last mile to a good campsite, when heaven declared war on earth. Every inch of that last mile was filled with ten thousand missiles of water. The lightning held off. We were already soaked, so we went for it.

I remember drawing the brim of my hat down close, almost over my eyes. I focused my view on the canoe bow and a piece of shoreline I could see out the corner of my left eye. Paddling through the downpour became a spontaneous burst of adrenalin, a primal love of life. Every nerve fiber in our bodies became focused on our goal. We held close to the shoreline, prepared to leap to the forest if the storm began to throw its lightning darts.

We finally gasped in sudden relief as we slid up to the rock shore of that second campsite. Pulling the canoes heavily up on shore we then turned them over, their bellies full of water.

That second day is now just a memory prodding us forward on our journey through the rain. But after eight days of threatening clouds scurrying across the sky, even the hardiest lover leans heavily on sheer determination. We are bone weary of keeping dry enough to retain warmth.

Perhaps it is the rain, or perhaps it is the broken canoe yoke, that taxes our love for this life of wilderness travel. The canoe itself is borrowed and weighs far more than it should. The yoke speaks that truth. It is my turn to carry it on the portage. Every time I balance it well, it crushes down on my head and threatens to roll me off the trail. Anger rises in my blood and I grip the gunnels with white knuckles. I am determined, I will not be defeated. Together we arm ourselves for the battle of this rain and this yoke.

We have entered a small stream. Marsh vegetation is an arm's reach away, but we have good water depth. The rain has finally gone and we begin to see the sun. Another tight bend in the stream just ahead slows our speed. In the lead canoe, Paula paddles in the bow. What happens next leaves me in amazement!

As they round the bend, Paula faces what she thinks is driftwood in the stream. But glancing up again, her eyes meet those of a bull moose, thirty feet away and closing in. With no place—or time—to turn, she and her partner, Pert, bend their paddles with frightened strength in a backward pull. The instant numbing alarm, wrapped in wonder at the sight of it, brings the moose closer in their minds. In these seconds of excited flight, our canoes become logjammed and lose all the nimble agility typical of the craft. Panic does not describe what takes place in those moments. Rather, I would call it awakening.

The moose, too, had an awakening, for it had not heard our silent approach. It too saw just driftwood moving upstream until human voices broke the mirage. What kind of fright or alarm rushed through its veins? What crazed thought may have flitted in and out of its mind? It could have crushed the five of us, left us broken. Instead, it turned and lumbered up a hump of peat moss toward the woods, leaving us alone.

The five of us huddle in joyful stupor. Of all the sights and sounds anticipated on our journey together, we never thought to breathe the very air of a bull moose passing. Something happened in the dangerous moment that I cannot explain. Tough eyes melted in the flowing stream and determination lost to the joy of being alive.

Occasionally, I see beyond myself to that magnificent, muscled animal that benevolently rendered to us elegant pardon. The loud breath from its nostrils, sized like silver dollars, and its rack of bone wave off all intruders. But in the leather hide and matted hair, and within the coat of water-darkened armor, must move the heart of kindness. Twelve hundred pounds of potential fury and not one ounce turned on a slender woman gripping a trembling paddle.

When moose move through bogs—like children in deep snow—the sucking sounds of their hoofs leave an imprint on my memory. This imprint only slowly fills again with muck and thick water. When moose appear, as if from another world, the sudden impact leaves me reeling and departed from my world of strain and toil. From the shape of the enlarged velvet snout to the coarse tail, the moose forms an unnatural presence on any landscape. That is, until it moves. For it moves through time and space with ponderous, disciplined dance. Its movement brings meaning to God's orderly creation. I do believe in miracle cures for heartsick people searching this world for a God to place them into a creation narrative of true and natural life.

Completed in Vast Array

Genesis 2 begins with these words: "Thus the heavens and the earth were completed in all their vast array" (New International Version). This summary statement correctly emphasizes the role of humanity in the creation account. We do not direct, we are not even one of the actors. We are here, put in place like scenery on the stage of God's design. Not that we are unimportant. But if we are to flourish within God's plan we must understand the beginning, for it scripts the entire length and breadth of life's story as we know it and all that we do not know. The point is this, being human—as defined by God—means that we serve no purpose but God's. Each one of us has a place of belonging within the network of life arranged and arrayed by God. This is the simple truth that children seem to grasp better than adults.

The truth of belonging is literally meant to define our way of life. Going back to the very origin of life we can find no greater depth of understanding, no more descriptive and prescriptive fashion of who we are. Every molecule of our body is animated through the medium of belonging. God's blessed Spirit of life moves within every brain cell and heart cell and cell of life within us, according to the design of our belonging. So the most natural and fulfilling joy in human life is to walk within God's creation, to talk amid God's creation, to touch and feel God's creation, to look upon God's creation, to smell the fragrance of God's creation, because this is who we are.

Belonging is not something to question, to rebel from, or deny. For this will leave us homeless.

I am thinking of the black bear and the loon, and remember that the Gatekeeper always allows my passing.

Now there was no water for the people, so they
    gathered together against Moses and Aaron.
The people quarreled with Moses....
    Why have you brought us into this wilderness?
      Why have you brought us out of Egypt?
        Why have you brought us to this wretched place?
And God told Moses to command the rock to yield its water.
    But Moses struck the rock with his staff.
      Yet the water did flow.
Those waters of Meribah where the people quarreled with God,
    God's holiness showed forth as liquid and flowing as the water.

Numbers 20:2-13
author's paraphrase

Chapter 2

Without a Wilderness Home

An Eagle Cap Alpine Meadow

Heat poured off the streets of Portland, Oregon, during the summer of 1972. Sweating bodies and restless spirits filled those streets. I was working as a volunteer for a church service unit along with eight others. We ran a drop-in center and camping program for inner-city youth, just the ticket to vacate the city in its most languid moment of summer birth pangs. We decided to escape to the Eagle Cap Wilderness in the Willawa Witman mountain range in eastern Oregon. Without serious reflection, we decided to take the youth with us. I was a nineteen-year-old novice of the woods and mountaintops. My love for the wilderness far exceeded my understanding. This imbalance has never really changed.

We arrived in the mountains amid sunny midsummer weather; the smell of pine trees coated us like molasses.

Even those city-raised teenagers sensed the excitement of mountain air free from smog. I still remember the first morning out, waking up with a layer of frost covering my sleeping bag. Manna from heaven it was to an early morning wakening, after having the slope of the mountain to lean into during my night's sleep. I rose to shake the sleep and the frost back into the cavity of my memory. Alive, yes, alive with the full power of a mountain in my legs and an endless trail at my feet. My companions joined me at the sound of the campfire cracking the dawn's light.

Two days into our backpacking journey we arrived at a crossroads, a fateful point of decision. It loomed as a moment we would look back on with both longing and regret. We found that as a group we were ill-matched. Some were impatient, while others were as plodding as plow horses breaking the dry gumbo of Kansas soil. We all needed a change of pace, so to speak.

Morning broke on day three and our goal was to reach Ice Lake by nightfall. Our group split up. Sid and Brenda led the athletic minded on a trail that took the long way around. Tom and I, elected as the front runners of the less ambitious, were to lead the rest over the rock and snow of a low mountain pass—shorter distance, same elevation change, and no trail. By the contour lines on the map, it appeared to be an easy day for the sod busters.

Our smaller group now numbered eight. Most of these were teenage youth, overweight and not expedition minded. Back in the city they had a certain television, snack-eating, couch-lounging attitude. Life there was not providing challenge, at least not challenge they accepted. This day, on the other hand, held the promise of spirits rising to the challenge of burning calories and flexing muscles.

As our friends disappeared down a well-beaten trail with condescending well-wishing in their words and hearts, we looked to our ascent. We were a crew of misfit castoffs on our own secret mission—to return to something lost long ago in the shuffling and rearranging of society. Hard knocks had added fat layers to the mind.

The first two miles we followed a kind of trail or deer path leading straight up the lower reaches of the mountainside. At times we were forced to make lunging boot stabs at the waist high ground coming hard to meet us. Good fortune brought us to a small glacial filled lake, clear down to its muck bottom; cutthroat trout glared at us from its depth. We rested and caught our breath; actually, we caught more complaints than anything else. It had been a steep climb. But following the verbal abuse, we looked up the mountain again, where we could confidently see our pass into Ice Lake and imagine a campsite full of resort-like potential. Already we could taste the clear water and dreamed of bathing briskly in the early afternoon sunlight. Perhaps we would have trout for supper and laugh at the late arrival of the serious minded athletes.

Of course, all this daydreaming ended as we started our serious climb toward the pass. The mountain sun baked into our bodies the slow reality of scaling rock scree with weighted packs. One step up and half a step slide before another reach upward, and so it went. Like walking in Sahara sand tilted on end, we became desert wanderers with choking fear rising in our gullets.

After an hour's climb I braved a studied look downward from where we had come. That small lake was now the size of a pebble, and I had the strange feeling of taking a swan dive into its magnetic depths. Restraining myself, I exchanged a cautious glance with Tom who looked as if he had just walked out an elevator door one floor above the building.

We went on as late morning approached.

Two near falls among our lumbering comrades brought bravery to an end and loosed the floodgates of serious fear. My second studied look downward and back convinced me that a retreat would mean a long series of free-falls broken by occasional boulders. What a terrible solution to a weight loss plan! We moved ahead slowly.

Somewhere in the recesses of our imaginations we could still feel the fresh breeze on top of the pass. But even this clouded vision disappeared as we saw the mountainside, ripped open wide, inviting us down into a gaping crevice. Running parallel to the slope of the mountain and directly intercepting our path, this canyon in the earth's flesh festered before us as a fresh wound and was ugly. I thought to see blood on its inner wall. Again I looked at Tom.

Tom and I held conference a short distance from the group. There was no way past the crevice and no way back down the mountainside. With map in hand, we looked at what seemed the only possible route, a route leading up a different pass high up to our left. Earlier that morning we would have scoffed at the rise in elevation and the risk to life and limb. Now, we looked to the high pass as our only hope.

We lingered in our conference and gazed through silent prayers at each other. And in those moments we sealed a pact that brought us close as blood. If we lost one of these friends to this mountain's embrace, we too would die, die a social death and become widowers of society. In our coward's heart we could not face the pain of death back home, and so we would choose the continual wanderings of woods and mountain streams.

Thus resolved, we led on up and to the left.

Granted the grace to live through the climb, by early afternoon we made the top of the pass. Finally willing to open the lunch pack, we dined in the thin air, cafeteria style. And I could not eat. Instead, I watched my friends free-fall to their death, and I repeated this image within my mind's inner terror. Also, I brooded in silence over what would come of our descent.

Tom and I no longer exchanged words or glances, for we

had made our pact and there was nothing more to add. Timidly I moved to a position where I could gauge our imminent descent. My worst fears relieved, I thought it passable. There was an exhilaration rising from the group that only comes after painstaking effort and hours of dread have ended. What could match the nightmare of where we had just been?

Packs on and feeling our way hand and foot through scattered rock chimneys and slanting shelves of debris, we slowly eased downward amid rising hopes. Concluding half an hour of careful rock work, we delighted in a snowfield that ended in a gentle curl. Out came the plastic tarps for the slide and I can still remember the frozen buttocks and crazy sense of freedom.

What remained of our day's journey was a series of gargantuan stair steps of mixed granite, carpeted by alpine meadows thirsting in the snowfield's wake. This alternating of rocks and meadow made the descent manageable. I relaxed my death hold on the pact with Tom, so I could breathe again the mountain-sweet odors.

But as can happen, relaxed minds sleep too heavily. Simple beauty became a trapdoor, and not a rock stair. What happened next, the lens of my eye and the exposure in my mind will always show my terror-stricken heart.

As I led the way downward, I marveled at the good reason for calling these mountains the "Alps of the United States." Sandra followed close behind. Here were the most green, lush meadow grasses growing up from a thin layer of soil overrun by rivulets of water throughout. I found myself walking on sponge cakes atop the world. Here and there bursts of alpine flowers decorated the green.

Nearing the end of the sloping meadow,I picked my footing carefully with eyes half focused on the upcoming ledge with open air beyond. I maneuvered the edge of a 300-foot drop to granite below with a pivot to the right and so recessed to a small clutch of boulders and scree. Turning,

I looked to Sandra to follow.

Coming on too fast and unaware of the danger, Sandra clipped glibly through that meadow toward the fall. As she realized the need to stop or turn, she began to slide. Soon she was out of control, with no hope of a pivot or sideways lunge, while I stood fifteen feet away—frozen, motionless. I could neither move or speak, my own terror wrenching my mind loose from my body. We were two people, helpless before life's ending. Sandra simply slid to the very lip of the rock's edge, which was wet and cold as the kiss of death. With feet spread, arms flung, and breathless before the plunge, her left foot caught a nick—or graced flaw—in the rock edge, holding her body against a silent flight. Yet the momentum of her slide still propelled her forward, and brought her, bent fully forward, to the balance point.

I am convinced that she was saved by her pack and by her inattention to detail. The belt to her pack was unfastened, not because of logic about the risk of a fall, but out of neglect. Nevertheless, the pack served as the vehicle to continue the pull of gravity as it flung out and over her head, allowing the weight of her body to remain atop its perch. For a second in time she stood motionless, poised over the too thin cushion of air, her pack draped over her and clinging by its straps to her trembling armpits.

Twenty years later, I still remember not thinking at all, like nothing in eternity mattered. I was but a dumb bystander at the gate of heaven or hell. And I have frozen the thought of her free-fall out of my mind forever.

Silently, Sandra and I knew at a glance that we would not speak of the incident. Words could only bring reality too close to manage.

Cry of the City

My youthful explorations of wilderness were like a knife

probing the abdomen of life. Overstated? Only if like so many others you disconnect the wild from the substance of life. What I did not know back then was how necessary these explorations are for the very nature of human life and for the life of our planet. Without a wilderness home, human experience becomes subhuman. When we place ourselves above the level of the earth, we court existence only within the mind of self. Thus we lose all connected and relational aspects of our life experience.

Admittedly, this definition is theological. For in understanding relationships as the primary function of life we invite the person of God, the womb of existence, into our reality. Only when God becomes real to us within these relationships can we know the experience of being human. Otherwise, we are all gods and accountability ends at our own doorstep. In essence, we have the potential to rationalize ourselves out of community and thus out of God's judgment and care. It is frightening to think that wilderness—for society such a low priority—may be one of the few ways back into community and into God's presence. Henry David Thoreau said it almost 150 years ago, "In wildness is the preservation of the world."

Are city youth who sweat through summers of asphalt heat really different from anyone else? How shall we judge them from our lofty seat of high rise or farmhouse? After all, any claim to higher moral or social status is the tube through which we are sucked back out of the community of this world. Any hierarchy that distances us from one another is idolatrous, for it places us above and in God's place. And it is suffocating, for it stops the breath by which relationships breathe. Yes, we are like the city youth in our need for a wilderness home and we are like them in our manufacture of other securities that cannot dispense the same grace. When will we learn that our journey to Ice Lake has to do with our attention, the melting of our ice-hard grip on self. The journey to Ice Lake is the journey out of self, not the search for an end to the sweat and hard work of a mountain trail.

The cry of the city is in all of us. For we all deeply long to connect with life beyond ourselves. The city stands as a symbol of human creation, a mirror that can finally only reflect our image. The gods of what we create become our one god from whom we claim our meaning. All of modern culture and society seem bent on claiming this meaning. Yet the search is endless and our cry continues. No amount of creating will ever satisfy our human soul.

Gabbro's Broken Quiet

They came paddling down a northwest wind. Aluminum canoes, noisy as ever, were drums announcing their arrival. They were young and alive with the dance of the wind in their hair, and so we watched their approach from the shore of our campsite. Gabbro Lake stretches diagonally from northwest to southeast, narrowing sharply to a small inlet where it welcomes the steady flow of dark water from Bald Eagle Lake. Our campsite island almost blocks the stream flow from Bald Eagle into Gabbro, yet allows a narrow passage off its southwest shore. Here the canoes met our view and grim faces returned our gaze. Most people traveling the canoe routes of northeast Minnesota and southern Ontario soon learn a respect for the expanse and grandeur of the place. Even those who struggle to comprehend wildness find something here on which to focus their appreciation. But this group was an exception.

This group included teenage youth with several leaders. We recognized the leaders by the lines of grief and apology marking their faces. We recognized the youth by their verbal abuse of the land, water, wind, and canoeing in general. As they came within easy earshot, these youth welcomed the chance to dump their epithets on some comprehending, though innocent, victims. Unrequested, the verbal attack reached our ears. High on the list of grievances (amid fluid cursing) were the lack of showers and the money they had spent to take their trip into misery. We greeted this chance meeting with silence, the only response that seemed fitting.

The water-stained rock sentinels on their left and right could have drawn their attention. The nestling of quiet waters in refuge against the wind could have drawn their attention. The gentle bend of the wide-leaved floating bur reeds passing under their canoes could have drawn their attention. And the nameless native peoples who for centuries before them nurtured spirituality from this place could have drawn their attention. But all that could have been fell broken on the bows of these canoes and these defiant, lost souls.

I clutched at my sense of reality. Inwardly, I reacted to their open and vulgar challenge to my feeling of home. I wanted to deny their words. I wanted to seal their lips and force their silence—not because I now questioned the truth of this place, but because I could not believe that these travelers were immune to the infection of wilderness. What had our society done to them? How abused must one be to stand in defiance of a lovingly wrought landscape of beauty? How could anyone, no matter the intensity of their pain, block out the smell of pine sap in moist air lifting off a dancing liquid surface? How could they not see the wraiths of glaciers marching from the north to sculpt the image of God on these rock columns? How could they not feel the wind breathing God's life into the forest animals and the fish beneath their canoe keels?

What had our society done to them?

I wept inside as the wind from the northwest filled the silence after their passing. Pine needles lifted by the wind skipped over the rock's rough surface and rested against my side. I felt so fortunate to be aware of the life around me. I knew we would soon be paddling straight into that north-west wind and I could only long for it. I wished to call these travelers back to me and give them a piece of their past, present, and future—wrapped tenderly as the petals of the lily hold the fragile disk of life within. We are this disk of life cupped tenderly by the shapes of spruce and alder, granite and metasediments, hydrogen and oxygen, spirit and matter.

When will we learn to call "home" that place where the narcissistic search for meaning does not abuse our youth?

On Knowing Home

The siren song of the wild casts doubt on knowing home. In this song is the note of truth shielded by the sometimes comfortable boxes in which we live. The way of society is the way of many illusions, a way that is normative and dulling. We must have life this way because this is what we can manage. One of the illusions we have lived with (quite literally) is that what we call home is something we buy or build for our security against the elements or against intruders. While this human invention appears to work well for some, others suffer greatly because home is not a haven for them. In fact, home may be where the intruder resides (as in the case of an abusive parent or spouse), or home may be where security disintegrates (as with divorce). Therefore, life itself fragments and splinters into isolated people we call individuals. Much of Christian thinking has unknowingly contributed to the "be strong," "be successful," "be American" routine of our culture.

The siren song of the wild casts doubt on our culture's claim to truth about home. And two Scriptures claim truths counter to culture. The first claim says that home cannot be something we buy. The second states that home is not something we build.

We read in Psalm 24:1, "The earth is the Lord's, and everything in it, the world, and all who live in it." Such a claim cannot be understood within a democratic, capitalistic society without a clear alignment to another allegiance. Even the very foundation of our sense of belonging (home) is changed from something we own to something God owns. If we are to truly make this shift, we become wholly dependent on God to supply our home. Now even in a material sense, it is God who supplies our security and physical comfort. This is no simple formula to add to our list of things to be thankful for. This is truth for how the world is. It determines the center of our lives and how and why we live differently than a materialistic world.

In Matthew 8:20 we read Jesus' words: "Foxes have holes and birds of the air have nests, but the Son of Man has no place to lay his head." God's human experience in this world was less settled than the creatures of the forest, more adrift than the birds of the air. Was Jesus homeless or was all the world his home? Was he actually "at home" while journeying through life? We humans make a lot of being settled and stable. Might we better find our comfort and security in our journey as did the one to whom we pray? If home is not something we build but something we discover on the journey, then we cannot lose it to a fire or mortgage company. We can only lose it when we get too settled, too tame, too comfortable. This definition is opposite to society's claim. But we should not be too surprised, because Jesus turned the tables on much of past and present human thought.

Of course we are always challenged by the question of those who would be comfortable. Must we actually take Jesus as the example of who we are and how we are to live? As long as we are settled people, we will always ask this question. But if not Jesus, who will be our model? Anything less leaves us back at our own doorstep, rationalizing and ratifying a way of life that is not Godlike.

It is good when a wilderness experience leaves us less settled. We experience this natural part of life too seldom.

To be drawn into a community of life apart from our own mastery, and to be conversant in relationships we do not control, is the only possible way to feel true acceptance, to know the kind of love that does not have to love us. This is why a wilderness sojourn is so important. It is one of the few times when we have such opportunity for an authentic relationship with animals and inanimate creation. Without wilderness, all the world is under our thumb and no community of created life is possible.

Also, without a wilderness home we run the risk of categorizing people much like we do other creation. Somehow we always end up controlling or being controlled—a sure way to a lonely life. The bitterness of the young paddlers near the southeast shore of Gabbro Lake that day was most clearly a cry of this loneliness.

Ima Lake Portage

The trail stretching from the stream, over a granite ridge, and down to Ima Lake's eastern shore climbs and falls in typical northwoods style. Repeatedly carrying a canoe does not produce tunnel vision, but an upside down "funnel" vision. I know the forest floor from about four and a half feet above the ground on down at a forty-five degree angle. Not the least serious result of this funnel vision is the occasional splitting of tree bark with one's canoe bow. Consider yourself fortunate if you have never equally damaged your canoe partner.

A few years back, while following a canoe route from Kawishiwi Lake to Snowbank Lake, I was pleased to find that we were the only group on this portage. Being early August, there could have been three canoe groups hovering airport-style, waiting to make the landing. My charge was a group of young adults. Two nights earlier we had weathered a thunderstorm to match all others. With no one hurt and with only minor equipment damage, I had confidence in their hardy spirits. Little did I know how I was to be tested on this portage.

We eased our canoes gently onto the small sandbank that announced the opening in the forest wall. In the moment before we began pulling gear and canoes onto the shore, we relaxed our tightened muscles—a luxury allowed at the end of a stretch of water. Actually, we were all relaxed since the day's travel had been light. There was not the typical quickened effort to load packs and canoes for the portage. The day was warm and I knew that Ima Lake, a campsite, and a swim would be waiting for us, even if we took our leisure.

The trail to Ima does not boast any strength-testing, rugged, uphill distances. It is a mere fifty rods, a rise, and then a weave through a bit of forest before the short descent to water.

But what a descent! Toward the end of the trail, as it bends down and to the right, a great grey rock buttress, ton upon ton of granite, opens into a narrow stair-like fall of broken boulders. As you lower yourself from ledge to ledge, the air in your lungs is thrust outward by the press of pack and canoe with every jarring drop onto steel-hard rock. To your right and left the lichened giant walls rise close about. With the feel of a cave dweller you enter a cavern that dampens as you go deeper. The last few steps before the water's edge are pooled with runoff from the matted vegetation above. You ease into these last steps, uncertain about which pool might deceive you by its depth and plunge you forward and bring you to your knees.

The narrow water entrance allows elbow room for just one canoe carrier to ease the craft into water three feet deep, and soon deeper. Perched on the water's edge and looking up at the looming giant rocks, I thankfully remember the generosity of the buttress for inviting me to drink at its entrance. Even on a hot August day the shade and refrigeration of the many layers of granite might refresh a sunsick traveler.

In those few moments before departure into Ima's open spaces one might also ponder the life of lichen. The community of fungus and algae, a symbiotic pair of stone chiselers, finds its way of life together on rocks everywhere in this land. No matter the six-month ice of winter or the pounding north wind or the dust-dry summer heat, the rock bears the banner of yellow-orange stain for its coat of arms. Proudly it seems, this splash of color boasts its tenacious grasp of knowledge of the rock. Lichen does know granite in ways nothing else does.

And so the final pause before the stone stairway affords a look at a complete ecology. It is cold perhaps, and still to our observance. But it is life all the same, and as such is another friend of the passerby.

I can call personal attention to the schooling from lichen on stained rock walls, since it was on this portage ending that I lost all patience and my sense of calm. The lichen allowed my advance into impatience, though I truly find it an embarrassment.

Our canoe group began this portage march leisurely. Politely, I chose to bring up the rear. As the last of our group began shuffling up the trail, we heard voices and the splash of quickened water. Seconds later three canoes slammed onto the sandy bank and ground the sound fully into our ears. The barking of their "sergeant-at-arms" quickened the pace of our group as the newcomers transferred from water to land assault. I was thankful to be last in our line, hoping to provide a buffer between the groups.

As I eased my way up the first hill I heard heavy, impatient footsteps behind me. At the top of the rise I half turned, canoe and all, to greet my pursuer. We exchanged hellos and I saw that it was the "sergeant" himself who was leading the charge. I briefly explained that my group was ahead and told him about the narrow exit of the portage. I added that our group would move quickly and asked could we please be on our way before they pushed past us. He agreed, although I knew his heart. Somehow inner driven, this heart was not well represented by his civility.

We caught up with my group as the first canoe was being loaded for departure. They soon got underway and our second canoe slipped into the water. As packs were moved toward the canoe, my trailing companion could wait no longer. He took charge of the situation. Forcing his way past me, he descended through our group as if his canoe bow was a bayonet.

Narrowly missing several heads, he flung his canoe onto the water, causing the defiant boom only aluminum can make. His loyal troops marched through the breech he had made in our group. We moved aside, partly from necessity and partly from astonishment. No two canoes could load and depart this portage at the same time, and so we chose to let them through without a confrontation. I sat atop a small rock ledge where I could contain my anger and watch the devastation.

Now I could see to whom this man was directing his orders. Two timid looking, middle-aged fathers and three stumbling teenage sons were struggling to keep up with him. One of the sons, still wearing his pack, stepped into the water, lost his balance, and plunged into the lake, dowsing himself and his gear. More verbal abuse flowed from the "sergeant." Somehow they managed to avoid serious injury and made their way onto Ima Lake, and went on to further conquests.

While others in my group began to recover from mild shock, I seethed in anger. My anger had grown from the time the other group's canoes hit the sand at the start of the portage. It gained strength with each pounding footstep behind me on the trail. It multiplied as "sergeant" shoved past me to get to the water's edge. It reached red hot when he nearly cracked the heads of my partners with his canoe.

And finally it boiled over when I witnessed the abuse dealt to the fathers and sons. I used my last bit of restraint to glue my lips together tightly and to hold my fists firmly to my uncrushable rock seat.

Once again I had witnessed wilderness being home to none. I cannot imagine the irreversible impressions of abuse those fathers and sons must associate with the woods and waterways of northeastern Minnesota. What frightens me even more is how I, too, lost all sense of my surroundings, all hope and peace, all patience of the lichen.

Will I ever be worthy of the solitude of this place? Dear God, may I return to your presence and find healing in your patient love!

Sinai Wilderness

We know relatively little of the forty years of wilderness wandering of the Israelite people, led by Moses. The life of the people would have been struggle much of the time; survival was uncertain. The hours passing to days, and days to years would surely test the faith of all. Our modern minds cannot image these years of wandering, for our minds will not measure such a term of homelessness. Imagine the thirst, the steady gaze on depleted reserves, no way to guess the nearness of the next oasis. No trail map. No synthetic gear of any kind, not even plastic dinnerware. Mothers' breasts would sag from the endless journey, while children died in the heat. Old ones whose comfort would have been to rest by a hearth on a Judean hillside, now could only dream of someone else's future and not of their past.

Anxiety for fulfillment of life's deepest needs awakened anguish through hopeless days and sleepless nights. There was nowhere to stop for long. Each stop was not only rest, but also delay and time snatched from dreaming, a cycle of violent thought resulting from unplanned resentment for the journey.

Is it any wonder that the rock was struck in anger? Is it any wonder that patience wore thin? Is it any wonder that God's presence was not enough to give them a sense of home? The waters of Meribah gushing forth were no easy symbol of a restive heart. The waters of Meribah flowed to an angry people full of longing for comfort and ease.

Here we have an honest narrative reflecting the nature of humanity, restless and unsatisfied. The human heart continually searches for a product, an object, a conquest, a security, a familiarity—anything that might temporarily fill the lack of meaning. All this produces a driven mind full of the tactics and anticipations of getting and taking. The promised land, the million dollars, the promotion, the new home, the waters of Meribah come in many forms for all people. And what both sophisticated and simple minds find is that one longing gives way to another and another, until life itself is fully taken up with the existence of want. Without being aware of it, our perceived needs become life's meaning.

The Israelites in the wilderness were a people surrounded by God's care—for their food, their water, and their defense against attackers, for the cloud over the tabernacle by day and the fire in the cloud by night. In the wilderness and far from being settled, their dependency on God was an ever-present part of daily life, and they loathed it. They had a constant drive to get somewhere, to gain the promised land, and to get on with life. Not unlike the youth of the city or the youth on Gabbro's southeast shore or the "sergeant-at-arms," moving on and moving up in life, they chose to mortgage the presence of God for the future promise of society's dream.

In simple words, a wilderness home grows from seeking and finding God in the journey. It means finding God's presence without our manipulations. It expands within as we look out on a clear morning at the waters and the trees and knowing deeply and sensing fully that God loves us in the morning, in the waters, and in the trees—and that God most surely lives in our thoughts and our hearts.

Without a wilderness home calendars and clocks rule the pace of life and show no mercy. We do not have the strength to stop our needful spirits. Without a wilderness home we are trapped, going around in circles in the Sinai Desert, as our inner anger overflows into depressed states of the mind and spirit.

All the while, God whispers in the wind above the waves and sings to us as pine needles fall in the breeze. The footsteps of God echo in the movement of deer in the meadows. God's fragrance lingers on wet leaves. All the while God beckons to us from the shadows of evening as God's face appears in our painful moments through blades of grass waving patterns undetected by the hurried traveler.

And Jesus set his face to go to Jerusalem.
  Some would not receive him,
  Some would only want to follow him.
He prayed at places along the way.
  He told stories about farmers and fields,
    About birds and grass,
      About fig trees and vineyards.
Jesus went from town to town teaching
  on his way to Jerusalem.
  He confronted the pious, he healed the sick,
    He ate with sinners.
He entered the wilderness of the lost sheep.
Weeping, he entered Jerusalem.

Luke 9—19
author's paraphrase

Chapter 3

On Entering Wild Places

Weathered Sentinels

Granite rock is hard—harder than most things we touch. It can also be colder than most things we touch. Mostly it remains impenetrable, without compassion for skin and bones. Granite separates off to itself, so that it might seek silence—alone and forever still.

Like granite, the human mind can shed much water and beat off many intruders. The human mind can become an impenetrable surface. Like granite, we can choose to become inanimate on the inside, allowing our relationships to grow rigid and to lose living warmth. Entire regions of the mind might await a warmer climate or a softening touch, without our sensitive knowing.

Few things grow on granite. To do so, they must intrude. A gnarled arm and a twisted trunk jut out from the granite. Though not a thing of beauty, the prickly needles of a jack pine tree proudly rise from its dwarfed figure.

In the northwoods, amid the waterways and granite ledges, it is not unusual to find these cousins to the tall jack pines of the forest. We might marvel just to imagine the trees' determined struggle for life in this place. Contemplate the awesome task of establishing a root system in granite. What human hands could never do, this little fiber of nature has joyously undertaken.

You see, there are cracks in the hard granite surfaces. Granite, as everything in nature, must be able to move—to expand and contract. So the crack that allows the roots to enter the granite is no flaw of nature. Rather, it is the grace of temperature change and the elements that provide this natural collector for water, dirt, and seeds. Thus, the tree becomes an ornament and a friend to the rock, adding beauty and furthering movement into life.

May the tree and the rock become symbols to travelers looking for ways to open and enter. What is hidden deep inside can crack open and spring forth into greening.

Basswood River

The long summer days were already shortening. A touch of fall could be seen in the scrub red maples around the campsites and portage trails. This was the last canoe trip of the summer, and I longed for a passionate way to say goodbye to the wilds of Minnesota. I eagerly awaited my companions who were driving in from the East Coast to experience the sights and smells of the northwoods for the first time.

On the first day of any wilderness trip, one may experience a full array of emotions. Excitement and anticipation rank high in the early morning hours. Wonder and joy intersperse as attention is drawn to small miracles of nature along the way. Yet not everything can be anticipated or planned or measured. Often there are hardships and obstacles to be surmounted. Challenge can become more than one bargained for, especially on the first day.

Our first day out was typical. Beauty was all around us and evident to all. The portage trails were tough, because canoes and packs weigh heavily on beginners. And the lakes provided a rhythmic paddling pace that brought us to our afternoon campsite on Jackfish Bay of Basswood Lake.

Not all first days appear to be what they really are. That night around the campfire we spoke of trails and water paths. Had I been on a different route? Evidently the day had not gone well for most of our group. This news hit me without warning.

In various ways, our group let us leaders know that the day had been too strenuous. One friend said, "I know the way back," meaning that this might be his choice of direction come morning if we planned to keep up ten-mile days for the remaining five days of the trip. How did he guess that was what we had planned? It was perplexing for us leaders, because we both silently felt that the day had been easy. We also knew that there were some tougher days ahead. What to do?

Wisdom prevailed, and we chose not to end the discussion that night. We could travel at least one more day before we had to make a final decision about shortening the route. We all slept uneasily, and I wondered where my passionate good-bye to the northern wilds had gone.

The golden sun wrestled with lingering gray-blue clouds as we sat on wet logs around the breakfast fire. The rain during the night seemed to fit the mood. No one ate heartily. Just before breaking camp I led the group in a time of reflection and anticipation. My subject was "letting go." Letting go of our personally-wrapped and tightly-fitted expectations would mean that anything could happen. What a new and unnerving thought! I could tell that new thoughts like this were not going to get us back to my dream trip.

We paddled in silence to the portage around Upper Basswood Falls. This portage can be long or short, depend-

ing if you want to brave some minor rapids on the
Basswood River. We chose the rapids and the shorter portage.
After playing in the water by the falls, we gathered for a bit of
encouragement and instruction on running rapids. Several in
our group were new to this game played in long, thin, and
weighted boats: Never get caught sideways with the current
and lodged against a rock. Never, never (if in that unholy
position) tip over upstream and into the current. And so on.

Because the water level was low, we could hardly see the
first set of rapids. The first three canoes went through with
barely a scratch, so as the fourth canoe headed into the current, I relaxed the muscles in my stomach.

Eighteen-foot fiberglass canoes with a straight keel line
and loaded with equipment and people, cut through the
water straight and true. But they take a long time to turn. In
a constantly changing current, maneuvering even a minor
set of rapids can sometimes be a challenge. And so our second morning out became the critical moment of the trip. All
memories of that trip seem to flow toward it or from it. At
the time, my canoe partner and I were perched on a flat rock
about forty yards from the rapids. We settled in to watch
and to judge that fourth descent through the dark water.

As the fourth canoe reached the middle of the rapids, I
could see they were in trouble. The combination of currents
and eddies had pushed them sideways. The thrill of strange
movement underneath them and all around them gave way
to a low-grade panic. Reason left the boaters and the
instinct to flee took over—but there are not many places to
run in an eighteen-foot canoe. During their panic, they
lodged nicely against a large rock that held them against the
current's power. Stuck as they were in the middle of the
stream, precariously balanced between a boulder and seemingly wild water, low-grade panic rose to a fever pitch.
Now reason turned against them.

In their panic the partners chose the quickest way out of

the canoe, which meant simply giving in: "Let the water in and let us out!" This decision led them to the forbidden action of dumping the canoe upstream into tons of flowing water.

I crouched on the rock and trembled, really trembled. I knew the tragic outcome, but I tried to deny it.

Because of the roar of the falls in the background, the scene before us played out like a silent movie. But the tearing of the canoe sides and the pop of aluminum rivets was loud enough in my mind. I watched the men disappear into the water along with their packs. Simultaneously, the river water rushed into the canoe, doubling it over backwards around the rock. I wanted to scream, but I did not have the strength. Somewhere inside I cursed the distance between me and the canoe. And I cursed the decision that had left me on the rock and useless to my friends in need. Mostly, I became overwhelmed with a numbing depression.

I cannot erase this scene from my memory. The setting is one of great beauty—mist rising from the falls and the wild river parting the deep forest. No amount of time will ever replace the marring of that picture. And I was responsible.

As soon as the way was clear, my partner and I sped to assist our friends. We joined them just below the rapids and I realized immediately that the canoe was not the only thing broken. No one was hurt, but spirits were drowned by the cold water's grab at the once light and nimble boat. Though I had no heart for it, someone had to begin the process of mending the broken things. I forced myself to speak encouragement. Then I forced myself to carefully study the remains of the canoe.

There was some hope for the canoe, though I could not sense it. Of the seven foam and fiberglass ribs, five were split. To our amazement the bottom of the canoe was not severed. Though there were major cracks and gaping openings in the sides of the canoe, all was solid up to about the three-inch waterline. The gunwales were partially torn and the rivets had popped, but they too had not snapped. The canoe looked critical, but it was not dead.

We worked carefully, almost tenderly, to get the boat out of the water. We spent over an hour drying and taping the bottom so that we could float it to the nearest campsite about a half-mile downstream. After setting up camp, we spent most of the day working on the canoe and hoping that we could continue our trip. With the help of a fiberglass repair kit, three or four tree branches, plenty of duct tape, and much patience, we finally felt satisfied that the canoe might float us through the week.

Patching up the canoe was the easy part. While we worked in silence, there were still severed spirits walking the campsite. Unspoken questions plagued us. Would the canoe float? Should we just cancel what was left of the trip? Who felt like doing the trip anyway? Who would pay for replacing our canoe? After last night's discussion and today's accident, was there any way this trip could get worse? Was there a way that we could ever get over the feelings of loss and guilt and depression?

Fortunately the recovery was not left up to us. As the day wore on, little glimpses of our surroundings began to penetrate our minds. Our campsite perched on the river's edge overlooked a section of tumbling, churning white water. The rhythm of pounding and swirling, dashing and splashing against anything in its path could only go unnoticed for a time. Water moves as eternal mystery and it is a seduction, as subtle as it is strong. There is a constant temptation to fall into the arms of a flowing stream as if it were a lover. Seduction had its way with us, though we could not yet tell it.

Autumn smells were just as endearing. It was still August, but the dry hot temperatures had brought down some of the golden canopy of leaves. Pathways were littered with decaying beauty. The rich smell of leaf odor, as it replenished the soil, further allured our senses. In a gentle afternoon breeze an occasional leaf fell at our feet or lay on our lap. It had become a majestic day and we learned of it slowly.

After supper I began to anticipate the evening discussion around the campfire. Would words again hold frustration pressed into images of expectations, unmet or shattered by the order of life in wild places? I was no longer even sure of myself.

Campfires, too, have magic, as light finds logs to dance atop and around. The shadows cast by the flames move fast and silently, dodging aging pines whose bark glows momentarily as they pass. A campfire can seem to wick up the experience of a day and return it in pulsing bursts, eagerly drawing mind and heart into its rhythm. As if a drought had ended, our spirits drew fresh water from the campfire's rekindling of the day. I was glad the dark could mask my face as I searched my emotions and steadied my voice. My eyes misted from emotion, not wood smoke.

I could hardly believe what happened that night. Or should I say, what happened the entire day. Voices around the circle of light felt warm to the hearing. Some felt salty and moist and I could share the feeling. Not one word expressed a note of disappointment. Again at night, I was surprised—but this time by love.

To reach this emotion had taken a great hardship. The pry of ice and boil of sun's heat had reduced that rock in the middle of the rapids to a welcome nestling place for seeds of human nature.

A Doorway Small Enough

Locating a wilderness area on the map is only half the story of entering a wild place. This half, the enticement to explore, boasts the material with which our inner spirits yearn to bond. The search for this bonding often ends without success. Even so, this is the easy half, but it cannot be truly found without the exploration of another wilderness.

The second half of wilderness blooms internally, and presents a greater demand. This is the shadow land that must find daylight. This is the place of protection and struggle. Here rock-like crusts block the new greening. And here we require weathered sentinels to post the way.

Too many wanderers seek their way in a new land without seeking their way in a new spirit. And too many wanderers seek their way in a new spirit without seeking their way in a new land. Either search leads to just half a discovery, and just half a discovery leads to self-seeking.

We all live with expectations. We constantly set goals and plot life's course. Sometimes we become so programmed that a moment cannot have value unless it fits into the plan. We have become too depressed to live. What a shame that life itself cannot be more celebrative!

And so here we have it, the dilemma of control. You cannot plan your way into wild places. So we ask, how then is it possible to enter into the wilderness? The only answer echoes from the words: Wild places are only wild because they remain unplanned by human minds. The terror within the human mind stems from the probability that unplanned wild places have the power to change us. But only if we find an empty place in mind and heart can we explore these interior and exterior landscapes. (I am indebted to Barry Lopez for the imagery of the interior and exterior landscape. His book is *Crossing Open Ground*, Vintage Books, 1989.)

There is more than terror waiting here. There is joy unspeakable. For the power of the wild takes us to a place that is worthy of our trust. This power will not do injustice. This power creates, never destroys. This power brings the possibility of new relationships that we have longed for since the beginning of time. And within relationships this power brings life itself. What then can it be that lurks past our scheming? That waits for us in wild places of earth and spirit?

It is a healing God who gives us dwarf jack pine trees to signal fresh cavities for bonding into a material and spiritual world.

Day of the Portage

A one-pound bag of M&Ms was hidden judiciously and deliciously at the bottom of the gorp sack: it was a treat for the end of the trail. Only two of us knew about it. Ordinarily a bag of M&Ms would simply be an addition to mix with other treats, giving us energy to last through the morning and afternoon. This bag, though, signified realized potential. It came at the end of our longest portage and honored the sign of our having entered deeply into the wilderness of both kinds. We were now five days into the trip that had begun with the breaking of the canoe. Completing this 300-rod portage—just one portage among seven for the day—meant we had survived almost a mile of lugging heavy packs and canoes through a forest on a trail that rose and fell repeatedly.

Lest it sound like a hardship tale, be assured that on this day only whoops and whelps of excitement broke the lips of the travelers and signaled the end to the trail. I was on my way back down the trail in search of a second load when the two youngest members of our group reached the end and lifted their victory song into the woods. It rang true in my ears; my feet glided over the pathway. What had happened in these recent days? Where were the sick emotions conjured from the depths of human experience? Why could M&Ms and a 300-rod portage bring us such delight?

Together we rejoiced in the accomplishment, ate our treat, and headed on to new adventures. After all, the day was only beginning.

Few trips have forced me to deal with such immediate changes of heart. Few trips have dealt such hardship and joy. I could not have planned a trip like this even though I might have wished to do so. More had happened than a simple change of expectations or a discovery of new ideas. This was entering a new land where things are not as we think they should be, but as they have been before us, and will be in spite of us. The most empowering thing that happened to all of us was the near destruction of the canoe.

Water had its way for a change, with both the boat and the masters of the boat. The energetic upheavals and glancing blows off boulders were the river's way of playing with the canoe. We experienced the river's personality with every back eddy, every whirlwind funnel dancing with sand in its brow, every curl with foamy crest. Every life-giving molecule being pumped through this earthen blood vessel—all had magic to give us.

Finally, we could feel the landscape of heartache, the crest of vision, and the valley of contentment. We tasted the earth while walking and sipped the songs of birds with morning coffee. Labor and sweat became glad payment for touching tree bark, still sticky with late summer sap. Fish whispered us to sleep and filled our bellies with the knowledge of ocean depths. All this lured us on, and yet we came to know only the beginning of the new territory. Mind and spirit, tree line and rain showers together underlaid the journey.

Walk to Jerusalem

From our stories about him, we might conclude that Jesus knew his journey's outcome: a cross and much suffering were the cost for a lifetime of giving. But it cannot be said that Jesus controlled the outcome. When he began his walk to the sacred city he too entered further into the journey of the earth. The hatred and violence of human life had long inflicted the cross of suffering onto the world of creation. Jesus could not have walked in more solidarity with the earth than that day he turned toward Jerusalem.

Through wadis and atop crested sand hills, with dry wind in his face, Jesus felt the suffering of the earth beneath his feet. For people had spilled blood on this land. The land cried out, as did the poor and sick of the city. Abel's blood had been given voice again and again. Roman soldiers occupied the land—as they did the people—out of fear and threat of death. Jesus' entry into the suffering of the earth began at his birth—an event attended by domestic animals in the earthen cave. Early on, he joined the land. He always lived as part of the dusty paths and the wind-tossed Galilean Sea. God of gods and a caring earth wanderer he was.

You see, entering soon becomes more than a way to begin a trip or a life of ministry, whether the journeyer is God or God-created. Entering is commitment. Entering is transformation. Entering is rebirth and cannot happen without a willing choice to relate in new ways. In fact, entering represents the new reality of being. It says that God now lives with us and distance is no obstacle to new life. Entering says that I am now present to life around me and that distances no longer define me. Rather, it is being present that defines me. This presence marks the beginning of intimacy.

Jesus chose the walk to Jerusalem because that was his nature. Entering takes on new dimensions when we accept that God entered this world, first in creating it and then in redeeming it from the death grip of human violence. God's entering signifies identification and wholeness of Spirit, of being one with the universe. We who would find many ways to separate God from creation must realize that in doing so we do not do God's work. We do not define God's heart. We do not know of the Divine entering at the dawn of creation. And we do not share knowledge of the divine reconciliation at the cross. And if, in our hearts, we truly separate God from creation, then we may have eternally lost God. For how could we selfishly preclude God from other life while holding God in our small hands?

Entering may be by a small door, but this door opens onto a vast community. By entering, God births a holy union. By entering, we accept.

Doorway to the Sky

The large wooden door opened slowly, creaking. We jostled our way through it and were greeted by a shaft of cold spring moonlight on the edge of timberline. Most alarming to our sleep-drugged ears was the sharp crackling of crusted snow under the lug soles of our boots. Suddenly, my senses snapped to attention and the reality of where we were hit me fully as bitter cold laid hold of even my covered parts. I looked around and beheld a view of the darkened shapes of bodies, buildings, and the few remaining trees. Mostly I saw snow, once white and glistening, but now covered with the darkness of midnight.

Our voices were but whispers. The silence carried by the thin air was overwhelming. Where there was not snow there was frost from what moistness the winds could blow. The frost made my beard stiff, as if gel had molded it into a winter style of its own. At that moment I was so glad to know that I held company with other warm-blooded creatures who were not stiffened by the long winter.

We began our climb of Mount Hood, Oregon's tallest peak, by stamping the cold from our feet as we tramped our way single file past the last recognizable life forms. Snow would be our only pathway for miles, and always at sharpening angles. And as the angle increased, the metal crampons gilding our boots became more comfortable.

We learned a "rest step," if it could really be called that. In those endless dark predawn hours we kept on the move, ever upward. But each step included a split-second pause as one leg locked into place at the knee. During this pause, the relaxed leg would dangle, limp in rest, though ever so briefly. And thus our steady movement kept the cold at bay and let us rise far above the large wooden door that we had opened but a few hours earlier.

We were ascending an escalator into the sky. In those blackened hours of footsteps on icy snow, the vision of rising above the earth was the only thing on our minds. We could not really see further than a few yards of shadowy moonscape. Still, we knew the direction, for it was always up—always the most difficult direction for tired legs. Adding to the difficulty was the irresistible urge to stop and count the dazzling little lights dotting the universe. But to do this meant lifting one's gaze off the uncertain and already dim staircase, and to risk stumbling into a literal mountain of hardened snow. So the stars had to wait, patiently, as we slowly ascended.

About one mile into the climb we reached a small warming hut. We crowded into the protection from the wind and gulped the high energy food that had frozen in our packs. The hut was little more than a dark shadow itself, but I found it hard to leave. I knew that the sun would first find us far beyond sight of this place and hours more into the moonless climb. As I moved again I could feel a deathlike cold seeking me from some distant galaxy. Thin, fluid fingers grasped my heels and toes, and inched up my lower back. I mentally imaged the caloric warmth of granola bars beating off those cold fingers and I quickened my pace.

There are times when it is easier to risk in the darkness, when we cannot see all the obstacles in our way. It is a risk to rise with a mountain in twilight and to dance on the peak of the world before the dawn. Courage may evaporate as the unknown gives way to the knowing of daylight. Sometimes the only journeys worthy of adventure are those we know in darkness. And so when daylight arrives we find surprise as numbing as the cold. Mystery has given way to further mystery—with color and dazzling and the knowledge that we can never return to a time before the journey. Our timidity is too late. The breathtaking view of where heaven and earth meet has engulfed us.

And so softly the light stole around us. We could not really know when it began. First it was pale and ashen, like the face of one ready for burial. But soon the east began to glow with a living light that the snow above us reflected in orange tones. This was a world of steep angles and bright white carpets, and we sought faraway sights in the mist of the valley below. I was overcome by a featherweight feeling, like a soaring spirit leaving its confinement for a morning song.

As we finally came within sight of the deep gouges that slashed open the mountainside and pointed to the summit, the steep humpback of Palmer Glacier gave way to the even more angled wind-swept ridges of White River Glacier. Opposite our single-file rise on a snowy ridge was a strangely captivating sight: extreme ice and rock scree, with fall upon fall of the mountain's rugged pockmarked scales. Here was rock too steep to collect winter snows; rock so bold as to show its naked figure.

Every chance I got I stole glances at the beauty of the naked rock, as inviting as it seemed calloused. It was here that I began to take in the full rush of the height by which this mountain maintained its authority to rule its valley subjects. The power it displayed crept up into my feet, even through those lug soles with crampons. I knew when it found the muscle and sinew of my calves and thighs, for then it leapt into my heart. I was captured and released all at the same time. This thing, this engorged rock growing under me, this pulse of matter pressured to the ceiling, held me like centrifugal force inverted. The thought of the millions of tons of mass that created this dazzling, lofty perch kept me suspended in a gravitational spell, while I also felt my wings strengthen as a young eagle taking its first plunge from the nest.

I dug each boot into the snow steps with the anticipation that each elevation rise would endear me more to the mountain and lengthen my new flight pattern. The sun was bright now, with a glistening that required dark glasses. At that height, the world was as clear as tap water running through crystal. The blue of the sky was popping out at me from brilliant angles. The air felt clean in my lungs. I was being romanced and my body was flushed with excitement for new intimacies.

The morning was growing long when we made our lunch stop. From this perch we sized up the last two sections of our climb. The first was a long, lifting hogback that posed no real challenge except that of staying on that long thin backbone. The second was a snow bridge over an open crevasse, and then a steep chute straight to the top. Lunch had little taste as I ingested the view. Behind us somewhere and not far away was a steaming crater, belching ancient desires of thirst for lava's flow. And I asked myself, "It can surely wait one more day?"

It did wait, and we moved quickly to rope up for the final ascent. Four of us were now tied together. We would either make it or not as a team. I began anew a careful study of the ice ax in my hand. I thought it a comfort to have and a bane to need. I hoped that no one would need to test its tensile qualities against the slope of that last chute.

The hogback proved to be a gentle climb and a good warmup for the real climbing ahead. The snow bridge was unnerving, as we traversed it individually, while anchored by the others in our group. The chute gave us the final test of our strength and will. Here we climbed a ladder with rungs of sliding snow. Our crampons delved deeply, searching for an ice hold. Every step up included a series of gasps for air. As each moment passed, so too the heat of the sun softened more of our hold on life. I looked behind me and down at the snow bridge we had crossed. It was 200 feet directly below us; beyond it was a free-fall onto hundreds of feet of that pockmarked mountain wall.

But it was in the last climb—the chute ascent—that I found clear glass windows opened onto a landscape beyond this earth. Though the snow was inches from my face as we crept upward, I became aware that the curvature of the horizon was mostly free of obstruction. And above me as well as around me was the still blue entrance into space unencumbered by my ideas of reality and life. As I labored to breathe, I breathed in the edge of an existence uncharted in smoke-filled board rooms. I lifted my eyes to what could be nothing at all or everything at once. I knew at the time that I had journeyed farther than ever before into God's universal will to life.

You see, this mountain peak became a gentle entrance into the wilderness of space. This soft white nodule of earth inched its way into the heartland of the atmosphere, with its altered pressures and different molecular densities. Here the chariots of sun rays rode the updrafts of earth's sweat and toil. Clouds of sweet succulence dropped far below me. I could imagine myself as a wanderer, in step with God's cadence of stars pumping through the galaxy, as life-giving blood pumping through our veins.

We reached the summit as a fresh cloud bank swirled in from the north. I walked stiffly about an area of snow packed hard by the wind and by boot prints. This area, the size of someone's back yard, was only the loft from which to catch the rush of cloud and to taste the air of the planets. This was a surface from which I could begin my climb.

Ever Entering

The weathered sentinels marking the entrances to wild places could be almost anywhere, but they are placed only where we find them with surprise. These windblown salutations of life exist, even though we do not notice most of them as we pass by. For an attitude of the mind allows or disallows our recognition of life's openings.

An attitude of the mind also allows time and eternity to pass without seizing a death grip on any one moment of entering. For we cannot possess the moment or the process. And yet, far too many people would hold onto a moment in time and live a life dancing on the pinhead of that experience.

Just so our image of creation, or God-entering. Must we seize the moment and dance it into numbing repetition? Or can we release the moment and participate with its unfolding? The one is to hold God, while the other is to be held. The one may feel secure, while the other takes us on a wild ride.

And just as creation can be a spiritual vision of God's continual entering, our world of spirit and truth becomes a succession of divinely creative acts. Nothing is the same twice, and no thing is without its newness.

In this we begin to see that entering is the ongoing event that gives life its animation. God never changes the creative process in order to make it less creative. And for us the climb is always the beginning. We may reach a level of interaction with the wilderness of our mind or a mountain, but the real relationships found in these places feed on new discoveries. This is the reality of becoming the opening: the open spirit, the open experience, the open vessel for God to nourish freshly and with celebration for the moment.

And so, to enter a wild place we are at risk. We court the likelihood of losing the virginity of our last encounter with God. We risk finding God in self-transforming ways within the lair of the untamed earth. And all this is exactly why we cannot resist our return to wild places.

Now God told Abram to go from Haran,
*   to leave family and home,*
*   to the land of Canaan where God would lead.*
And Sarai and Abram and Lot left their home together,
*   with God's promise to bless them,*
*   with God's promise to bless all the families of the earth.*
And they traveled to the land of Canaan.
*   They passed through the land to a place called Shechem,*
*   to the oak of Moreh.*
There God appeared to them and they built an altar.
Moving on to the hill country east of Bethel,
*   Again they built an altar to God,*
*   And invoked God's name.*
They journeyed on by stages toward the Negev.
And together they left their home,
*   with God's promise to bless them,*
*   with God's promise to bless all families of the earth.*

Genesis 12:1—13:1
author's paraphrase

Chapter 4

Living the Journey

Campsite in the Past

Not long ago I revisited the islands of Little Saganaga. The lake surrounding these islands changes with the winds that blow across the surface, scattering patterns of waves like flocks of birds merging in and out. The drop and crest of surface water sees motion as its only natural state.

And so it is with the shoreline, the bays and jutted points. Shorelines—rock-buttressed as they appear—move in chorus with pine boughs and lapping, fluid waves. Wetted and glistening, these caressing boundaries signal for the moment their special outlines of the restless lake. And light itself, which gives us a vision of the calm or fretted surface, casts the scene with fickle color as often as we blink.

The waters and the shoreline welcome me back, while the islands still hide their secrets of the lake's shy figure. It was late spring; a cool breeze lifted off the waves and I headed for the sun rays that were bathing a large sloping rock with their warmth. Here I rested and unpacked my lunch. The last day and a half I had been paddling and portaging, an honest and earnest effort to reach this place in the sun. As I ate slowly, I let the sun reach tenderly for me in my contentment. The world around me drew me in. I was once again a living presence sheltered within the life cycle of Little Saganaga. This sheltered feeling was in sharp contrast to the stress addiction I hoped to leave behind. This was a safe harbor, for the rotation of basic elements and the seasonal changes forever renewed the welcome here.

After lunch, my canoe bow once again parted the waters between close growing island pines. I lazily dipped and lifted my paddle and dipped again. I paddled into the breeze and softly into the interior of Little Saganaga. Its body of cold clear reflections mirrored the adornments of crystal just as I remembered from years past. Here on this bosom of womanly grace was a gentleness buoying my canoe hull onward to memories and a healing future. The afternoon was ours together, the lake's and mine, and so I moved in the pace of the sunshine while two friends became reacquainted.

Pulling the canoe on shore by midafternoon, I looked for a campsite with character and a view of the lake. Satisfied, I staked my territorial claim with colored nylon, hoping not to disturb the restive, natural beauty of the rocky tree line. The sun would set across the lake's span and I thought this rise of rock would be the perfect place to wish Little Saganaga a pleasant sleep. But for that moment it was enough just to finish my sheltering activities and to smile at the rain-swelled clouds changing once again the surface of rocks and water alike.

I camped that night and the next on the shifting space of Little Sag's eastern reach. The water showed me its boulder-strewn bottom. The daylight hours brought the splash of rippled waves and the frequent return of rain splash. I found the peace of mind I had lost in an earlier life; a settled comfort released the reigns of my pensive mind and I could depart that dwelling into the gray morning of the third day.

I pulled my paddle in grateful arch through the clouded sweep of sky and lake that had become one on that morning. It was one of those days when the light does not want to waken and play dancing music. The fog whispered in my ear with the lethargy of the dawn. Air that could not rise to its full height was held low by the weight of moisture. I was launched, dreamlike, into a clear vision of another time and another trip through Little Saganaga.

On a whim I turned the canoe south toward a campsite from long ago that was still in my heart. Though it was time to leave Little Saganaga, I wanted to pay my respects to when time stood still within the relationships of my world, mine and Little Saganaga's. So I weaved between islands and rock outcroppings and into a seemingly forgotten bay where ghosts walked and spirits of fish and flying birds knew my name and called to me once again. The spectral shapes of rock shorelines here breathed a long-ago air while they watched my entrance into this sunken hollow echoing the past decade.

The wind was still, as if it could not remember a time so long ago. The quiet was a hushing quiet that dared me to rouse it with water noise, but I could not. As I neared the campsite the trees along the shore threatened to turn this scene into a county fair ride that would make me dizzy. I felt disoriented—but it was only my spirit, unsure of disturbing the past.

I eased the canoe hull to where it could nuzzle the rock shelf. I docked on the ground that I thought could wish me its welcome. Pulling the canoe on shore, I knew in an instant that Paula had slipped her hand into mine. Ten years ago we had been here together, just the two of us wanting to make this scene ours forever. Now as I walked, I left footprints for us both. I swelled inside with emotions enough for two, and I touched this place for her with hands unfelt here since she lay upon the open green and fingered grasses to clothe the bare soil.

I walked about with one foot on solid earth and the other in my dreams. I could only half know which time dimension would bring reality back to me. And I moved about that campsite with more than morning mist from clouds wetting my view, for the swelling had become dampness and looked for release. How I wished we could share again those moments and relive the smiles and tender love of this place back then.

I let myself down easily onto the lap of granite beside the water, and I replayed the time Paula and I sat together, nestled there, watching the sun part the trees on a little island offshore. Amber bursts of light came out from behind the pine boughs as if they were fire kindled in the heart of root and trunk and arched branch, and even the needled whirls of treetops. Suddenly screams pierced this display of day-ending grandeur, like arrows piercing our beating hearts right down to the hardened core of the rock foundation underneath us. Our attention was drawn upward to the cries of winged warriors drawing battle lines in the sky, their talons as sharp as unsheathed sabers ready for the kill.

Inwardly we withdrew from the call of distress and outrage. But visually we were breathless at the sight of a herring gull and a bald eagle wheeling about the amber sunset as if they found it their time to lay claim to birthrights before the ending of the day and the close of mortality. These two dipped their struggling bodies to within thirty yards of our neutral zone on the ground. We watched them as the dark gray wing tips dodged the curled, bladed beak on the snow white head. Feathers appeared to wrap both bodies in aerodynamic armor that lightly graced the fighters, regardless of the contortions they went through in their twisting, churning, wild flight.

The gull had little or no chance to withstand the power of the eagle. It was not long before its high-pitched complaints could be heard from a distance; it had no will left for a prolonged conflict. The eagle, without a contestant for territory, soon drifted high and left us reliving the drama in our minds. We could not stop talking about the beauty of the amber-framed near collisions and tearing feather balls in the sun's afterglow. It was some time before we left our gaze into empty space and directed our attentions to camp chores before the coming of the dark.

I wrested myself from the past long enough to step into the woods where we had pitched our tent ten years before. What was most amazing was the clarity of those past images. It was as if I was dreaming the present while living the past. There on the forest floor was a small clearing and again I let myself drift easily into the reality of the long ago dream. . . .

Shortly after midnight Paula and I were slowly awakened by the marching drums of the distant heavens. For another hour we waited for the coming storm. It seemed to inch across the still air into the upper chambers of Little Saganaga's bed like a slow intruder for whom stealth is the only means into a calm stronghold. But with each measured and timed lightning bolt came the searing flare of further advance, and triumph thundered its glancing blows upon the lake's surface. As the storm neared our sheltered wood, the booming blasts of thunder reverberated through every particle of tree or ground or human bone. Tent poles seemed to quiver in the black night from the creeping, shrouded monster with a voice like pure pulsating power. Neither Paula nor I said a word, but within that tiny nylon coverlet we lay shoulder to shoulder and hip to hip, pressed hard together by anticipation and fear.

Finally the storm shrouded the air directly over us. As

we waited for the storm to break, mere seconds felt like life-times. And then the blow we most feared landed. Deafening roar and brilliant light laid our hearts bare in that instant; the orange ceiling of the tent glowed as the light of the sun itself. The sure feel of death launched us with the lightning into each other's arms, into an embrace worthy of being the last.

Because of the trembling in our bodies we could not mis-take death for life. With dust-dry mouths, speech did not come readily in the return of the blackened night. We simply held one another until the trembling left us, praying all the while for the darkness to remain. All around us the storm continued its slow-motion intensity, but there were no more deathlike blows. Within our warm embrace, driven by love and terror, we clutched at the meaning of continued life together, and we allowed the slow pondering of the storm's pardon. We had only now to listen as it marched on in search of travelers perhaps more prepared for eternity's journey.

The storm could be heard long into the waning hours of the night, and sleep would not return to us. The gentle light of morning came with a lazy drizzle as we packed up equip-ment still soaked from the heavy rains of the night. The world looked strangely like a mirage of clouds hanging low to hide the damage visited on Little Saganaga's tender figure.

We slipped the canoe into the calm of the bay as rain-drops sank into hiding under the surface of the water. As we began the renewed voyage with easy paddling strokes, I also pondered the single breath of life that could empty so suddenly. Inwardly I wept from a new discovery of love for Paula, so deep as to go beyond any temporal bounds of breathing or living. She was seated in the bow and I studied the dark green outline of her rain poncho as the morning lingered and her movements ordered the day. . . .

Stumbling out from my trance in the woods I moved about the campsite, looking for more artifacts of the earlier visit. But I also knew that my time here was over. Another campsite waited far away on Lake Polly. My reluctance to leave shadowed me like a haunting portrait of Paula hanging just out of sight among the trees, or the taste of her kiss lingering as I passed the campfire ring. I could not help but grieve for an earlier time, for a relationship so pressing that it now wanted back in my mind and in my body. I wept openly, shedding my past innocence and proving my humanity to the ghost-filled landscape.

I left that place, amazed at the magnetic yearning of soul for moments so precious as to overpower the present, and even time itself.

Moving Water

Sitting close enough to a river or stream to see the individual droplets of spray or the single strands of water as they burst over rocks can wet a person on the inside and moisten the dry seeds of life. Leaning, prying, drawing, and riding the current of that same river or stream may bring about a revolution of warring emotions, tangled like a web around one's caution. Water is a restless spirit. It shares its spirituality with the world around it.

Many times I have paddled across lake after lake in search of something not lost, but also not found. And then I would catch a glimpse of it as I remembered a long-ago trip into a different countryside. I would ponder the reflection amid the search. Why do we look back with different glasses and see meaning more clearly from this telescoped perspective? Why is it that the present seems to be filled with delays or boredom, while memories can linger larger than this present life? Could it be that water spirit has overtaken us and we are one with the flowing currents of hydraulic gravity? Perhaps we are the wind blowing in circles and sweeping across the river's pallid surface with intermittent bursts of uncontrolled energy, driven by an energy source that lusts for creativity.

To the casual observer, it would appear that humans are meant to command the quiet times, the settled experience of rest, and the luxury of calm. Surely we have this aptitude of bodies draped in comfortable surroundings and hearts set on stability. Seeing the world as it is today, we could conclude that the highest human achievement is to get more than we create, to sit in a passive posture gained in the past and reap continued returns from wealth or fame or injustice. It would also appear that surges of human energy serve only to allow us the freedom to loiter. Take, for example, the person who punches the time clock for forty years only to gain a string of Saturday night drunks and eighty vacation weeks spent floating in a cheap motel swimming pool. Or look at the executive officer of a multinational company who retires to state of the art pampering on every level of the human sensory experience.

These examples may be the extreme, but they provide a caricature for the driving force of desire. We all want to have it easy, to win the lottery of life. To push ourselves into new discoveries induces change and discomfort; therefore, this push becomes for us a temporary hardship withstood for the gain of rewards lavished and well deserved.

So which are we? Are we water-born spirit or sediment at the bottom of some backwater cavity? Are we made up of memories or present adventures? Once again there is no easy or simple answer, and certainly no answer that is final. Each of us carries this question with us on our own journey. And the most perplexing or perhaps radical discovery comes when we realize that both the memories and the adventures, both the quiet and the hardships, are born of our journey. The journey births and transcends both. Life's meaning is neither driven energy nor lapping luxury, but a confluence of slow and fast water, always moving to a fundamental gravity pull, an overarching energy source. God's Spirit blows where it will.

My memories on Little Saganaga's shore became an enlivening moment along my pathway. The love and terror I felt in my earlier visit to that place profoundly deepened my knowledge of inner haunts until then unexplored. At the same time, my sense of self within an ever-changing environment of caring for Paula became more understandable and yet more free of definition. The sequence of time lost its importance with the coming of blowing Spirit and spray of Spirit, whose elements laid bare the interwoven process of two lives threaded together.

This realization gave me the energy I needed to turn the gate wheel of a mountainside dam, flooding new rivers of unheeded caution and creating new cascades of spirituality. If water is a restless spirit, then so am I.

Journeys are not always continuous. We can always stop the movement, and we often do. Stopping poses no threat as long as we know we are still on the journey; as long as we know that life is the journey or that the journey is life, as long as we know that even the resting gives meaning to the journey and so continues a movement of soul. This type of life journey expects the unexpected, makes new discoveries, and welcomes a change of plans. Here lingers a traveling spirit, a wayward daughter or son knowing only the reality of blossoming, knowing only the truth of resurrected life, knowing God only as unknown, and eager to step into the presence of the One on the move.

Surely Christians might learn from their own stories of God's behavior: God in the wind. God in the still small voice. God in the burning fire. God in the act of mercy. God in the claim of justice. God in wrath. God in love. God in the infant birth. God in the healing Christ. God in the suffering servant. God in the oppressed. God of the empty tomb. God in us. Or plainly and simply, God incarnate.

We Christians might awake and claim obedience to anything but a changeless God. God is both constant and ever new. Our God comes to us as unsettling Holy Spirit because we always need to be renewed and sent packing, because we have usually thought of home as a location instead of a partnership in exploration. Our deepest desires of security and well-being far too often become objectified rather than relational. We want to halt the journey for a week when a day will do. We want to build or buy or maintain wholeness, when it is at best not our endeavor and certainly not a way to God. Wholeness of body and spirit can only be received from a God on the move; a God who surprises us into new ways of wholeness.

Far too often Christians become uncomfortable with this arrangement and choose a more stable God. After all, stability is a value undergirding much of Western culture. Some Christians would rather take the biblical stories of a radical and inbreaking God as their stable creed in exchange for the journey. The irony of getting comfortable with stories about an uncomfortable God escapes them. They choose to make the stories what we call Truth, instead of entering the story through the words of the One who said, "Come follow me." Do we really think that this call means only for awhile and that the radical nature and power of the story ends or diminishes with the close of Revelation 22?

The idea of journey, as we have been using it here, remains at odds with those Christians who say that the Bible is Truth and mean that it is literally a book of facts that have become our creed. I am not saying there is no truth or fact to be found in the Bible, for we do have in the Bible much historical data and a deeply moving revelation of God. What I am saying is that the Bible describes a God that cannot be contained in a book. The book itself was not written to contain Truth, but was written to invite us into a life given over to God. With Sarah and Abraham, this God moves us from the Land of Ur to Shechem, to Bethel, to the Negev, to Egypt, back to the Negev, back to Bethel, to

Mamre, back to the Negev, to Beersheba, and finally, to the cave of Machpelah. As Abraham and Sarah were taken up into the journey, so are we. In reading the Bible through the eyes of faith, we leave the confines of closures made of mortar or words. In so doing, our faith is surely placed into a living relationship that can only survive while we are travelers and aliens in a land where God always brings us new revelations.

To say that the journey with God can be exciting—even thrilling—and that it can be filled with pain, is to acknowledge our unknowing. To choose a journey instead of a creed is to trust a faithful God who touches us with love, in and beyond the pages of the Bible story. Because *we* are now the story!

Shoreline of Crooked Lake

When I see Crooked Lake, I see a vast corridor between uneven walls, an art gallery hung horizontally with boldly-painted canvasses revealing depth and color. I have floated these hallways in company with others, looking beyond the gunwales of any still life. Hundreds of miles of shoreline link together the outline of those corridors. One cannot claim a knowledge of Crooked Lake without first embracing and welcoming a restless spirit. God coyly waits for the traveler who is willing to risk surprise attacks from the enclaves and island haunts along the lifelike display of Crooked Lake's expansive green-clothed body.

Dark water decked with white converges upon the eastern shore of Crooked Lake, which sits at the confluence of the Basswood and Horse rivers. From their overquenched forest beds, rivulets add a million trickles of jeweled drops that seek unity with the surging masses of liquid energy. This water rushes through three different openings and down twelve-foot drops, greeting Crooked Lake with white-on-white foaming madness. This, life's beginning for the lake, comes in at dizzying speed. The momentum surges relentlessly day and night, springtime and summer, fall and winter, year after year. But if incoming life would just slow and halt for a portion of time long or short, if the Basswood and the Horse would descend some other rocky drop and rivulets find another path in the sea, then Crooked Lake's body would stiffen and stagnate. If the winds could only billow the surface of other lakes, then Crooked Lake would begin to die of stillness. And if Crooked Lake depended for just one day on yesterday's flow of water, a twenty-four hour portion of the life cycle could never be regained.

A distant bay on the Canadian side, about fifteen miles from this genesis, can only be entered through a narrow channel lined with lily pads and water shield. We have followed the eagle into the heart of this bay and lodged on nests of fallen pine needles. The bay seems to be the nest for a large island lying in its middle. The island nest may have the potential to hatch some new life of its own. And so we settled on the eastern shore with a view to the setting sun and the island's eastern bank. The wind lapped the water constantly against the stone shore, which in turn glistened with the moisture. It was a comfort to camp beside the water, to know that we were travelers in the good company of this water traveler, to know that in the morning we would awake to a new and different water surface—for the lake never sleeps.

To fall asleep to the sound of moving water, as if it were swirling about the tent walls and buoying the ground, brings to me a sleep of peace, for I am assured the pace of the universe. The water moves and so the recycling of moisture throughout my environment will sustain my morning. There will be coffee from a steel cup, rinsing water for my face and hands, milk on granola, and rain from pregnant clouds. If for one day the water to and in my body ceased its march, depending instead on yesterday's flow, my sleep would bring no morning. And so, water music is the best kind for sleeping. Travelers on the journey depend on it.

Awake or asleep, the flow of God recycles my life and I take it for granted. I need surprise attacks from God to help me see moving water, and to feel it in my heart's pumping. And so I explore the shores of Crooked Lake, thinking that maybe God will pounce. Sometimes God leaps my way and I only remember it the following day. Sometimes God hides and I am lured further into the back bays of Crooked Lake, only to discover that I arrive too late, with only a birch tree to tell me that God's hideout keeps changing. Sometimes I do not want to look, and then God takes me like a storm and I am tossed across the water to places strange and infrequently visited.

I fail to see what God expects of me except to renew my search of Crooked Lake's secrets, to double back and look more carefully at what I missed. But when my paddle blade swings wide around the intended turn, a deep movement of channeled force seals its hold upon the canoe hull and upon my fragile body with it. In the same instant my heart trembles in my fingertips, frantic at the loss of my own power. Now the movement of water terrifies me while all my strength is set against the current to no avail. Caught as a wanderer destined to die suddenly, I cannot bear to open my eyes to the rising mist of Curtain Falls as it swallows me whole. The shock of pounding water, thunder in my ear, lightning stabbing my free-fall, and bone-crushing wood-splintering impact on jagged rocks—all fully terrorize my soul. I am dying at the bottom of a pit filled with the alpha and omega of Crooked Lake's heaving aerated blood.

Time creaks by, like a slow wheel turning inside my broken body. Even as I lie helpless I sense movement. And the movement hurts me, rubbing raw against the places torn open by the rocks of Curtain Falls. I cry out repeatedly, pleading for a time before the falls or at least the cessation of the water's pull. Every moment I am certain that the pain is unbearable and that God has now asked too much; that God has pounced too hard, and that I have not survived.

Sure that no human could live through Curtain Falls, and giving over to death's blows, I expect to sink quietly amid the rubble of river bottom and lodge within the jaws of some cavernous crack in the rock floor. Though conscious thought comes and goes, I gradually become aware that I am starting to float. I am pressed upward and downstream. The ride downstream becomes a long, gentle healing and I can begin to breathe again and feel a small amount of love again. After weeks and months of adjusting to new swirls and twists in the currents, I empty out into another lake, a new lake.

I would like not to think about other lakes and other falls where God will take me and open me. I would really like to become intimate with my new lake while I look for surprise attacks from God that still allow me to double back now and then. But I know that the water keeps moving and God too never settles down in one lake. And I know that my long process of healing has left me ready—strong, actually—for the journey ahead. Each pain of life's changes has brought God's sometimes raw power to mold me. I have become part of the journey; I am with Christ in the boat on the windswept, stormy Sea of Galilee. My life may be unsettled, but I always share the experience with divine company. (The crash down Curtain Falls is an imaginative way of describing the spiritual journey, not an actual real-life event.)

Uncomfortable Faith

Comfortable. This word connects all the strands of middle- and upper-class values. Comfortable is also the death mark swept across the forehead of faith. For Christians within wealthy societies, comfortable becomes their reason for defining a benevolent God. And in this scheme, to be comfortable ratifies and justifies religious experience; it proves the validity of faith (as if faith can be proved by any means).

Within the context of this padded-pew style of stoic worship, the paradigm of journey meets with uneasy glance. For journeying takes effort, and inevitably brings discomfort, even pain. Journeying means new beginnings and it means unanswered questions. Journeying means getting off the padded pew and walking into the company of God, perhaps dancing to the music of worship. Journeying means that conclusions are temporary and that hand clasping replaces finger pointing. Journeying is listening, not telling. Journeying is not comfortable.

If life were meant to be comfortable, we would have muscles that grow strong with disuse. We would have minds that expand without new understanding. We would have happiness within our boredom. Our spirits would soar without fresh fire. But we know that this is a lie.

But if we know the lie, what stops the journey? Why do most Christians wish to remain comfortable? Why do most of us remain quiet in our Sunday morning pews and hold so desperately to past beliefs? Why is it hard for us to keep our hearts open to the ongoing story of God's redemption, including the redemption of our belief system?

Can we blame it on our comfort and say that we have sold our searching faith for recliners and fundamentals? Is comfort really that strong a motivator that we would close windows to God? Do we just get lazy? Or is comfort only the cover-up?

Could it be that we objectify faith because we truly

cower from uncertainty? And perhaps we cower from uncertainty because to face it we would have to enter the darkness of our doubts—doubts about self and about God, doubts about the goodness of life, doubts about the goodness of our loved ones, doubts about the goodness of the earth itself. To search the closet of our doubts would mean risking everything that we hold dear. Our worldview would likely crumble and we might not recognize the new world, for we would have lost ourselves in the darkness, like a closet without an exit.

Is it possible to stay in that closet of doubt? Can one hope to get out once one is in? We all say no to the journey when it becomes too frightening. We are so unsure of ourselves when we get beyond the comfort zone that this isn't always a conscious choice. For example, can we allow the possibility that there is no God, that we have made God up in order to keep out of the closet of doubt? Or can we allow that God does not conform to our standards? Can we allow that our form of worship is less than adequate for nurturing divine and human reunion? What if we have succumbed to a rigid, lifeless manner of biblical interpretation, a gasping hold on a prejudiced Christ with Western white, male dominion?

Could it be that we are wrong? Dead wrong about faith and life and God and us and earth and past and present and future? Yes! All that we have protected and shielded from doubt, clouded over ourselves and God, all that is static and objectified truth is likely our very worst nightmare waiting for the distant day when too late we shudder in horror, knowing that we lived the lie and feared to doubt. We actually lived in a worse darkness than uncertainty, for we did not live truthfully. We did not tell our doubts and share our love with risk. We did not cry or laugh or scream our anger. These were the only true emotions and these were the only real moments to share them.

We have been good at believing the God of the future,

but we have not accepted the God of the present. Or we have cataloged God with the past and distanced the present. Therefore, God incarnate has no personal meaning, for gut-wrenching compassion flows a stride before or behind. If God incarnate took a personal turn and burst upon us, we could only thrust open that closet door of doubt. Any system of belief would shatter in the instant of flaming presence. We would doubt our very soul. How can we imagine that we know the secrets to words written thousands of years ago when we cannot shape our own true words of passion here and now? Or why think that we can somehow limit God to other worlds than the one being created before us this very moment?

Comfort is not our problem, for its sweet surface only coats the terror that lurks in our hearts. We live, locked in chronic fear, pampering an image of God, because the incarnate God would make us doubt, make us change, make us move, make us enter reaches of the mind that flood with a trembling spell of terror. We do not really want to know the ways in which we have lived wrongly, judged harshly, and especially not how cowardice has led our march of days in this land. We do not really want God to be so real that our images of life are destroyed even if . . . there is life beyond our images.

And so now the time has come to say that we do not know, that we fear living this present life without answers to so many of life's questions, but that at least we want to stay with it and grope in the darkness. Can we just feel our pain without sugarcoating it? Can we doubt our soul and give it up to nothing or maybe, just maybe, to God? Can we reenter the journey and let go of the belief system that has until now kept us locked up and locked out of movement? Can we cry our love for someone who may not be there for us? Can we weep for the injustice that may be ours? Can we risk finding our heart and viewing its emptiness? Can we drain the soul of all content so as to spread open before a God who may never swell new shape within us?

Finally we discover the origin of faith. For faith begins when we get on with our journey: exploring our doubts, living our pain, and facing our fears.

And finally, we are present to all the possibilities of the journey. These possibilities are relationships, not truths, for the journey is all about exploring connections with natural life around us in countless forms.

Our parents' faith, the biblical narrative, the search for security in a frightening world, yesterdays' beliefs: all fail to witness to a real God who transforms fear into love—unless the story of our life has its own continuing narrative bursting open all the doors that otherwise close off our relationship with the God who is.

The God who is what? The journey is the answer.

And God said to Noah and his family:
    I now establish my covenant with you,
        and with your descendants,
        and with every living creature that was with you—
The birds,
    the livestock,
        all the wild animals,
            every living creature on the earth.
Never again will there be a flood to destroy the earth.
The rainbow is the sign of the covenant I am making
    between
        me,
            and you,
                and every living creature with you—
                    A covenant for all generations.
                    A covenant sign between me and the earth.
My covenant is established between
    me,
        and all life,
            on the earth.

> Genesis 9:8-17
> author's paraphrase

Chapter 5

Friendships Stored in Earthen Vessels

Primal Scream

The lazy flow of the Kawishiwi River ebbs past a slightly overhanging rock face decorated with paintings from the distant past. Etched drawings of some fish oil/iron oxide mix point the moccasined pathway to human story in step with Kawishiwi's past adventures. This same dark red art fingers the location of a campsite across the water channel, almost within hearing distance of the artist's happy labor.

The campsite itself appears blocked by a boulder fashioned after the arched back of a diving blue whale. Only a little water filters through the opening between the rock and the west bank of the river. But from the outer ring of the campfire circle, perched atop the lifted bank, you can meet the river's gaze from north to south while contemplating both past and present life there.

We settled there one lazy afternoon to soak up the quiet of the pine trunks rising from the silent earth. It seemed the only place where we could linger in solitary awareness of our existence outside the limits of time. So with nothing to do but exist, I moved slowly to the forest's edge where I could peer at the angles of reflected light off the ebbing water.

I lowered myself onto the bit of grass spread in a thin layer that ventured just outside the bounds of the towering forest canopy, an extra touch of western sun its goal. Without even a whispering breeze, the afternoon slipped by unnoticed except for the increased slant of the sunbeams. Trees stood perfectly still. Water moved, but sounded no verbal passing. The silence was deep, as if to bring back to life the movements of the artist's hand in the painting across the river. I even sensed satisfaction in ancient expressions of thanksgiving written on the rock. After two hours of this silent repose, I thought I might grow tree roots—as if becoming a permanent, clutching sentinel would seal my commitment to honor those restive fibers of living spirit within the rough pine bark that were teaching me their calm.

Suddenly, excited movement on the ground drew me out of this quiet euphoria. I heard a rapid attack of sound, amplified by the still air. Like a cavalry charge at dawn, the pounding staccato of small padded feet ignited the calm with a burst of energy. My eyes riveted on the object of blatant disregard for the peaceful woods. At first shocking glare I saw no intruder, but an instant later the furry blur of a red squirrel shot out of the bush and into the clearing. Half a leap behind the squirrel and pounding out its own blur of fur, rushed the fisher. Both animals, oblivious to anything but this life and death chase, ripped through the middle of our campsite. They shot straight for the river and my position, while I turned in amazement to greet the sight. Ten feet away they swerved hard to their left and down the riverbank amid boulders, grass, and lapping water. It had taken only two seconds for them to pass in and out of view, but those seconds filled me with the intensity of their struggle. Within those two seconds their bodies melded into one, their leaping became one leap, their lunge for life a single hope.

That hope was tentative at best for the squirrel. Seconds later its scream split the air. I had never heard a squirrel scream before, and this scream chilled the marrow in my innermost bones—that part of me that shapes my self-understanding. I shivered in silent regard for the last agony of the squirrel and the hungry lust of the fisher; one, not two, tragic fates of nature.

I could not resist the pull of heartfelt emotion. Slowly, even timidly, I moved in the direction of the scream that was as real in memory as it had been in the actual hearing. It was the repeated screaming in my mind that drew me, with magnetic lure, to the death scene. I could see blood dripping from a lifeless form, the little heart now motionless, but still warm in the fisher's jaws, and I could somehow feel the terror announced in that primal scream. All this pulled me forward toward the rocky pile where I knew life's giving and receiving had occurred.

I never actually saw the fisher again or even what might have remained of the squirrel, for the final drama had taken its course within a deep rocky cleft where I was not allowed entrance. But I stood close by that granite framed door, whispering solace to my soul, claiming the right to life and mourning death's advance on the squirrel. As I touched the rock entrance and felt the pulse of the day succumb to the cold night, I felt my own heart falter. I held to that tomb of finite knowing as if to grasp the hand of spiritual transition making its move from an earthly plane.

Perhaps it was their leap near me or maybe it was their infectious intensity. Maybe they startled me out of my interior self so as to thrust upon the chase my own race with death. Or, more likely, their vulnerability unlocked my own and let me into their wild world where I had never been before. Though one rarely sees a fisher, I think of them quite often. In my frequent sightings of red squirrels, I now sometimes stop to visit.

Minn Lake Acquaintance

After paddling fifteen miles of the Maligne River—including portages around rapids—and bushwhacking my canoe through a quarter mile of thick forest, I entered the north arm of Minn Lake. I was met by the shallow drop of water signaling Minn's slight, but challenging, elevation change. After a long day, even that slight change pushed me almost to my limits. To get the canoe up that current meant using my last bit of strength. I then settled into the slight breeze on the lake and challenged the small wave action rippling toward me from across the water. I slowly gained speed, hoping for a quick trip across the lake.

Then it happened. In an instant I was frozen in space, lodged on a crusted piece of granite two inches under the waves. The bright sun had beamed its deception into the marsh-stained water while I had drifted away from reality in the steady beating of tired paddle strokes. Maybe crossing Minn Lake was not meant to be, or then again maybe it was my final testing for that day. Regardless, I nearly plunged headfirst into the water. It took every wiggle and controlled heaving that I could muster to throw the canoe into reverse action in order to dislodge, as well as to keep some dry dignity. Grateful for the miracle of lingering buoyancy, I cautiously parted the remaining waves southward and paddled on to a small island home for the night.

It was such a relief to reach the island that I nearly forgot I was alone, really alone. But after an hour of unpacking and loitering about the island, it all came back to me. I had been alone for the last eight days, paddling a wilderness of water. Tonight would be no different, barring the possibility of invasion by sky divers, desperate for the last of my gorp. That prospect seemed unlikely and the thought signaled that I was dangerously close to having a hallucination.

As the recollection of my solitary status returned, so did a portion of my energy. I explored that bit of island before preparing supper. Nothing unusual came of my island tour, but I was drawn to the repeated screech of an infant bird nested on a neighboring island. It turned out to be a baby bald eagle trying to fill its belly without help from its parents. With that discovery, I settled down to cook my supper. The eagle could not share the meal, but the invitation must have been carried by the wind, for soon a guest arrived.

Often in the northwoods a gray jay will swoop down on a campsite looking for a free bite, sometimes even resorting to pillaging a weary traveler's meal. But this guest brought an unexpected splash of color: some white, some yellow, some black in finchlike array. I was surprised by how casual the visitor—a male evening grosbeak with an appetite for fellowship—was. He perched on a dangling lower branch of a red pine tree close to the fire ring and eyed me from beneath his yellow mask.

The crumbs from my supper must have looked like a tasty substitute for his normal diet of insects and seeds. He cocked his head from side to side as if he wanted to see me from multiple angles.

I was lonely for a conversation, and so I spoke to the bird. I invited him to dine on my leftovers, and I wished him well. But the bird was unsure of my intentions. As I took a slow step backward, I persisted with the soft tones of well-wishing. And after a few moments of uncertainty, the bird dropped to a rock by the fire ring. I held to my hope of this companion, knowing that in one wing beat he could be lost to me forever. I continued to address my delight in his presence with speech that seemed to draw his attention between his gulps of crumbs. In my own mind I imagined a sort of response from the bird, judging from the knowing look in his eyes and his increasing ability to relax in my presence.

As our friendship grew, I tossed additional bits of granola his way. This met with his approval and gave me more time to appreciate the perfect beauty of his form and movement. I studied his costume design and choreography, and I forgot my loneliness. This guest of mine, little larger than a sparrow, taught me things about color, about balance, about quickness, about timidity, and about bravery. I saw in his dark eyes the kindness of all songbirds who fly across the surface of life only to decorate and celebrate beauty and song. Sure there is the chase when death and life mingle, and songbirds too know the hardships, but the warble of a grosbeak lifting from pine branches sings my heart to sleep.

The grosbeak ate his fill. I was glad to have hosted the meal and to have given a token of kindness. I heard no thanks offered from the bird, though I understood the thankfulness within his breast as he looked one last time into my eyes, the windows to my thankfulness hidden within his own.

I was alone again when the bird departed, but I knew our relationship had been put right. How do you measure the significance of a little bird? Perhaps we measure it best when we learn that we cannot.

Breakfast Thief

Guiding a group of teenage boys in 1987, I chose a canoe route along the shores of Crooked Lake. These boys proved to be an energetic group, and the first day of paddling put us at a campsite on the southeast end of the lake. We made camp, cooked supper, and ate our fill. The evening proved to be delightful, even for tired bodies. So after supper we explored adjacent shorelines and islands, and discovered a small stream and waterfall tucked into the hidden reaches of a darkening forest. Content and drained of all daylight strength, we collapsed upon our sleeping bags that night and slept heavily. Morning would come soon and we had plans for an early start.

Our goal for day two was to delve deep into Crooked Lake and seek one of her distant bays for our wilderness solitude. So we rose from our sleep early and built our breakfast fire in haste. We packed our equipment and readied our canoes by the water's edge. While the water on the fire came to a boil I lowered our food bags from their airy cradles out of reach of hungry, furry things with claws and teeth.

I make a habit of keeping all food undesignated for the current meal at a safe height of ten feet above the forest floor. But that morning I chose to cut corners and save a bit of time. So with the group's best interest at heart I kept all the food down, stowed it carefully by the canoes, and coiled the ropes. Then I joined the others for a quick breakfast.

While the Cream of Wheat and coffee settled in my stomach, I cleaned out my cup with some loose gravel and ambled over to the lake. There I dipped some water to rinse the dirt from my cup. (Keeping the lake water clean of any food scraps is a priority.) Breakfast had been relaxed, reminding me also to relax and enjoy the coming day. While I had my back to the campsite, the canoes, and the food, I leisurely cleaned every speck of grit from the edges of that steel cup. I even gazed out over the lake's calm surface, pretending to float with the air above it and across it in calm, pallid movements of my own. My reverie kept me from noticing the scene unfolding a mere twenty feet behind me.

As I patiently tended my eating and drinking mug, a black bear silently invaded our camp. There were nine other humans milling about the camp as the bear sniffed its way toward the food. Any one of the others could have flung cooking pots, screamed, or in some way raised the decibel level to an uncomfortable pitch for the bear. The other adult in the group spied the bear first as he sat with a few of the boys at the fire ring. My calm, collected co-leader responded to the furry visitor who was after our sweets by mumbling a quiet "bear" in a disbelieving tone. Because he could not believe his eyes, no one else believed his speech. Precious seconds ticked away as the bear followed the food scent.

Finally, one of the teenage boys spotted the bear and wailed a loud cry as he leaped toward the woods. With the fever pitched scream of "bear" in my brain, I spun around and jumped for the food bags, knowing at the same instant that I was living the nightmare that had always motivated my cautious hanging of the food. The bear could have been a giant and I would have felt no fear—not because of courage, but because it happened too quickly for my brain to catch up.

While leaping, I surveyed the scene before me. The bear was twenty feet away and hunched over the food bags. It had seen me whirl and knew that competition was on the way. I was at a disadvantage since the bear was already drooling over its prize. My one thought was to get to those food bags first. It never occurred to me that my cause was hopeless, that even had we started at an equal distance from the food, the bear was in control. I yelled out some half-baked warning cry as I hurdled the remaining distance between us. Still not thinking clearly, I did not have a clue about what I would do if the bear was unwilling to give ground. Even after a full summer of guiding canoe trips, I could not have seriously hoped to separate a bear from its peanut butter. And so in the final second the bear was left to decide the conflict, since I was acting without reason. Typically, under pressure, animal sense makes better sense than human sense. Thankfully, the bear was acting like a bear. With lightning speed it snatched a food bag in its mouth and exited into the forest.

At this point, most rational people would have collected the remaining food, organized the departure, and sighed in relief that no real damage had been done. But I wanted my food bag back. The bear was on the run and my brain was still back at the lake. Since I could still see the bear's behind ahead of me, parting bushes and tree branches, the chase was on!

The first twenty yards were mostly open woods with only scattered underbrush. Both the bear and I sprinted this distance easily. But then the forest thickened and the ground rose up into a hillside covered with thumb-sized dead and dying balsam fir branches poking their way into my face and hair. I lost sight of the bear. As I broke my way past the balsam branches, over rocks and boulders, around several dead trees, and steadily uphill, I kept telling myself that any second now the bear would come to its senses, realize its hopeless situation, and drop the food bag. So I labored on about fifty yards into the forest and up that hill. I imagined that the bear was terrified, trembling out of control, and wishing I would speed up so that it could surrender with a white flag held high in its right paw.

At last I had to stop and catch my breath. Oh, how faltering strength can prove itself a safety valve. With a moment of heavy panting—and perhaps a fresh flow of oxygen to my brain—I began to ponder the meaning of that chase. How much did I truly value my life? Would teenagers understand my self-sacrifice on behalf of their dietary needs? Would my family honor this selfless act? While sifting through these thoughts, I began to notice how alone I was feeling. Why were others not leaping through the woods by my side, cheering me on? Finally, I appraised my situation and brilliantly deduced my need for a reality check. It was past time to admit my defeat and be gracious about it. I wished the bear well and hoped it contracted only a slight case of indigestion.

Halfway back down the hill I was already laughing at myself in an excited kind of way due to the adrenalin brought on by the bear's presence. I still did not like losing the food, and I knew we would miss it dearly later in the trip, but I could not help bubbling over with the rush of chasing a black bear through the woods. I wondered what it had thought of me leaping at it and pursuing it like a mad man. Had it been afraid, did it know that I meant it no harm, or had it laughed at all my human antics? I suspect it only gave me passing thought while hunger drove its mind ecstatic over the contents of the bag. In choosing the food bag, it knew to pick the lunch bag will all our peanut butter and honey. The bear had followed its nose and had chosen judiciously, and so he ate better than we did that week.

While musing about the incredible quickness and beauty of the bear, I sensed a gnawing pain inside. My stomach complained with every step back to the campsite. Then it hit me. I was getting hungry for lunch.

Song of the Rainbow

The animal world is unpredictable. I do not have an animal mind, though at times I have wished for an animal heart. If I could, I would sing to animals a song of understanding among the species. I would want the melody to eulogize the speed of the tiny red squirrel, the cunning of the fisher, the brazen beauty of the grosbeak, and the triumph of the bear. Most of all, I would weave a line of harmony about the human longing for understanding. It has been our loss as much as theirs that we do not sing together.

I think of the man and woman who find distance a consolation befitting the relationship of dominance. This is the only possible handclasp for those who reach for one another from differing heights. So how can intimacy blend the two into one? How does a king become a pawn? How can love scale an altitude of control? Simply put, these things do not happen in our world. Relationships retain their arm's length distance and we believe accordingly. Controlled distance replaces intimacy, and oneness is redefined to mean something about superiority of race or sex or species. All this time, the woman and man are left with a longing they neither express nor comprehend. Differences are obstacles to faith in one another. And even in the trying they fail to know life's secret treasure buried in their definitions of self and other. These definitions hide the true meaning of existence. These definitions foster the misconception that others are to be defined by our standards.

But the buried secret has something to do with release, of giving the other over to the freedom of their own soul before the gates of heaven's dwelling on this earthly stage. The secret may linger just beyond our knowing and beyond our mental pictures scrawled across the faces and figures of those we love or desire or cherish for reasons of our own. The secret may fly in the whirlwind of God's activity and not in our own. Could it be that whatever value we place on the shape and destiny of woman or man grows within too many confines of heart and mind, even at the times of our deepest sense of open charity?

Perhaps we limit others when we least desire it until the time when we live in a world beyond human definitions. It may be that we only sing harmony, while God sings a spontaneous melody of joy. And if the song of life blooms from within God's heart, then only God knows the value of woman or man. Only God knows the potential for human release into the divine value system for all species.

Thomas Merton once wrote, "Every moment and every event of every person's life on earth plants something in their soul. For just as the wind carries thousands of winged seeds, so each moment brings with it germs of spiritual vitality that come to rest imperceptibly in the minds and will of all. Most of these unnumbered seeds perish and are lost, because we are not prepared to receive them: for such seeds as these cannot spring up anywhere except in the good soil of freedom, spontaneity and love" (*New Seeds of Contemplation*, New York: New Directions, 1961, p. 14).

It is wonderful to think that throughout our day, God could be found in the simplicity of every moment, that somehow right now a process of spirituality germinates within us. Just as surely, it must sadden the heart of God to know that we may never water the seed, and that it may dry before the living takes hold of us.

Pause a moment. Look to the moments we share with unfamiliar creatures. Perhaps the wisdom and the nurture we typically miss in these relationships reflects our inattentive spirit. Perhaps Merton is exactly right when it comes down to chance meetings in the forest. Imagine then what we may have lost—and what we may yet lose—as we continue our ladder-climbing ways. What if the value we place on furry and feathered life forms defines us more than them? What if our value judgments have little to do with God's? Then what? Could it be that our spiritual journey through this life is severely hampered by the limits we place on divine care for God's creatures?

Christian thought has not generally found much time for speaking to the issues of the community of all life. This in itself is sad commentary on how we continue to center our faith story around the human experience. Theoretically, we should know better, but we too seldom think theological thoughts about the implications of our everyday actions. We do know that our faith story speaks clearly on this account: God is the center, the Creator, the Sustainer. Our story just as clearly tells us that it is God who grants value to all creatures. It is God who establishes right relationships between the species, not us. In fact, it is the human part played in our biblical story that seems bent on destroying life instead of giving life. If you will, we tend toward undoing what God has done. This is a frightening thought for those who cherish a right relationship with God.

If all this seems unfamiliar to you, let me remind you of the Old Testament tale of the flood. In Genesis 6—9 we find a theological, not a technical, account of how God decided how to deal with the corruption and violence of humanity.

The entire world was threatened by our insensitivity and self-aggrandizement. The people had thrown off the yoke of God's way in this world. We had chosen our own pathway to self. Our determination to become "little gods" nearly brought an end to life itself. The accuracy of this ancient account should be judged less on the details and more on its application to our current global crisis. This story's validation can be witnessed repeatedly within our history books, and certainly is confirmed by present lifestyles.

Even so, this flood tale is not about us, not about the animals, and not about the tears of nature raining down for forty days and forty nights. At its pinnacle, the story of the flood is the story of our God in anguish, of our God deeply pained by destructive human behavior. This is the account of God's soul-searching, of God's agonizing love affair with the world. This is the tale of divine grace flowing from the same compassion that at an earlier time gave birth to the universe. Does it shock us to think that human history is not centrally written in this story? Does it disturb our easy theology that centers on fictionlike characters staging a play before our children's eyes with cute pictures of animals and boats?

God is the focus and the agent of action. It is God's heart of hearts that is throbbing. God writhes in wounded brokenness, bleeding internally from our plunder of relationships. This might certainly cause us to look at the soul of human ancestry. And this is the story, a mind-blowing concept of Eternal Divinity risking all on the choice of a second grace. Now, perhaps we can begin to fathom the depth of knowledge here that converts every angle from which we stare into the eyes of a wounded world. The flood story, once a religious nursery rhyme, now shapes our internally hemorrhaged self-understanding according to the boundless, wounded compassion of our Creator. Our worldview now must develop from our knowledge of God, our self-knowing from God's experience with anguish.

God chose to recreate the world. God chose to place divine hope into a renewal of the community of life with humanity still the flesh and blood emblem of divine charity. God's way was a way of starting over, of grace enough for all life forms to breathe the air of worship, drink the water of consecration, undergo the baptism of covenant. For it is in the faithful action of God within the context of supreme dilemma—faced with the justified ending of creation, faced with the near total corruption of evil, faced with a violent rabble of human disobedience—that covenant gains its meaning. God's covenant in Genesis 9 finds its validity in the compassion of recreation. God's covenant is established because of, and out of, God's nature. The flood story tells us who God is, and therefore sets the agenda for right relationships according to the covenant of our revealed God.

Now we can begin listening to the distant voices closing in around us from the many green and blue landscapes containing questioning faces within creaturely habitats. For the story of the flood carries the proclamation of God's bonding to life and living. This making of divine covenant in Genesis 9 claims God's bonding to all life forms: animals wild and domestic, all the earth, and Noah with all his descendants. What is distinctively omitted in this account is any dominant role played by humanity within God's covenant. In fact, there are clear statements of God covenanting with the earth, and God covenanting with creatures of every kind. There is no indication that God's bonding with creation is in any way dependent on human mediation. Once again, we must realize here that God is acting, and that God's compassionate grace is not given primarily to humanity. God's grace is certainly not dispensed to creation through us.

The power of God to make the covenant takes center stage. The structure of the biblical passage makes this clear through repetition. Though different words describe it, this theme is repeated at least ten times within the same number of verses: God promises lasting relationship to all forms of life, including the life-giving earth itself.

Rather than disappointment in this account, we can experience great release from feeling that we humans are in charge. We can take great satisfaction in knowing that God orders relationships, and that we may fit into this order if we choose. I hope we will choose to fit God's order, for our field of play on this earth is wonderfully wrought with nearby companions of God's design. We have before us the chance of a lifetime, for we are invited to step out of hierarchy and into companionship. We are asked to realize that our faith story does not support our previous claim to rulership over God's creatures. We are brought reluctantly into a transformed reality. We are to live life fully within creation, not outside it or above it. We are given yet another chance to live where God has placed us, and this place can be the only place where spirituality grows sincerely out of a covenant community where leadership is servanthood based on God's example.

A trilogy of right living is unveiled in this Genesis 9 covenant. Suppose we raise it up from a restless sleep and stretch the stiff muscles of spirit waiting for expressive movement. This eternal promise, this guaranteed certificate of assurance, this lovingly delivered bonding by God, establishes the covenant between God, humanity, and all of life. Three separate times in this passage the trilogy of God, humanity, and all of life is expressed as a united front for how living is meant to be. God makes the commitment to faithfulness. God proclaims fidelity to this three-part harmony that is meant to blend into one anthem of praise.

So why are we not singing? Why have we choked on the chorus when our strong voices could blend into the delicate song of creation joy? To abandon the trilogy of covenant life has cost us so much, more than we will ever know. Without the song of creation in our hearts we are left to sing alone.

We have not only lost a hearing with the earth community, we have stepped out of tune with divine covenant that orders the tempo and the verse of living. Though we still might relate to God in a personal way, this way lacks the full array of orchestral resonance, as if singing our solo could imitate a symphony. Without entering deeply into the symphony of creatures great and small, every aspect of the human experience diminishes. But no part of our being suffers more loss than our spirituality, for here is where life's meaning draws sacred breath from the passion of friends.

A symbol of promise lies in the heavens high above the community we touch, see, hear, taste, and smell. This symbol arches across the stage of the universe while gently floating its fingertips to caress and unite our crusted planet with its dream of creation. Our faith story proclaims the rainbow as the signal to sing joyously and in chorus. Let us take great comfort in the living truth of God's activity. May the rainbow forever be our symbolic invitation into God's universal hymn of worship.

Moments of Expectation

Occasionally on wilderness journeys I leave the hilltops and lakeside panoramas and excuse myself from my companions to find a time of solace in the forest. My destination is perhaps a berry patch on a distant ridge or maybe just a clump of pine trees secluded within the protective embrace of undergrowth. I seek out a quiet spot of ground upon which I might rest from the distractions of a traveling spirit. Once I find this place, I sit. That is all. Nothing else is needed, for everything is provided. It is my time and my presence and my choosing that was previously lacking from the scene of integrated listening.

While sitting on the earth I become the seed itself. Planted there, I take the time to grow roots that pump into me the very genesis of receptivity. Whether rocky or moist or fertile soil, it does not change the downward movement of my opening and the earth's, for this is a search she and I share within the mind of our Creator.

As I sprout new life, I am welcomed into the search for light that occurs as naturally as roots hunger for water. Light that would glance off my nose and fill my hair with a sparkle will also enter the veins of the plant community in order that energy might widen the rings of growth into the production of more seeds. I laugh as I sense the presence of ongoing creation. My ticket to this concert falls from my pocket and into my hand.

There is a creative presence here and I share its emotional reunion. All about me, life seems correct. Seems satisfied. Even seems fulfilled. And that brings me easily into my own sense of filling. I cannot actually see the connection. I cannot actually feel my roots entangling with sunken cords of trees. I cannot actually hold a light meter within green leaves. But I fully understand these things to be the compassionate proclamation of covenant. I clearly see through eyes of faith and feel through roots of faith the holy fulfillment of God's promise.

No thing is nurtured outside the promise of friendship if we listen with our hearts to our story of faith. No fleet-footed friend escapes the swift activity of God that spans planetary existence. Every one of those chance meetings in the forest could infuse our spiritual future.

Shall we not ask again why we humans strive to sing alone? Shall we not let go of our value judgments placed on the tender heads of songbirds? Shall we not finally recognize God's covenant as superseding our will to climb above our place of birth?

My body moves awkwardly into dancing steps. But I flit above the floor with grace and acrobatic detail as my mental choreography steps off in motion with my winged supper guest.

Now as they were on their way, Jesus entered a certain village where a woman named Martha welcomed him into her home. She had a sister named Mary, who sat at Jesus' feet and listened to what he was saying. But Martha was distracted by her many tasks; so she came to him and asked, "Lord, do you not care that my sister has left me to do all the work by myself? Tell her then to help me." But Jesus answered her, "Martha, Martha, you are worried and distracted by many things. There is need of only one thing. Mary has chosen the better part, which will not be taken away from her."

Luke 10:38-42
author's paraphrase

Chapter 6

Simplifying the Adventure

Beginning

Whole potatoes. Big carrots. Onions. Ice chests hauled out of canoes by their plastic handles. I have watched many times as people loaded or unloaded canoes as if they were U-Haul trailers. Going into the wilderness does not have to be simple.

But it can be. And keeping things simple can bring much of the teaching of wilderness to bear on life back home. So much depends on how one begins to plan and dream and gather together necessary items for the dreaming.

The trip began somewhere in our heads eight months before the magic date. By six months before the trip, the gray outlines of the plan had taken recognizable shape. We were going! And in some mysterious way the following six-month waiting period revolved internally around our anticipated rendezvous with wilderness. And it was that anticipation that could have fueled the fires of indulgence. We could have spent a fortune on unnecessary gear and bought a chef's gourmet package of freeze-dried delicacies. "If we had the money" was the operative phrase, because we truly did not have the money. In those days we begged and borrowed equipment. Anything but stealing was considered a legitimate means to get what we needed.

Starting out the way we did cost us little more than the gas money for driving to the trailhead. Looking back, I am grateful for experiences like this that taught us to be creative, to pack light, and to throw out non-essentials. I will admit to having learned various lessons about packing too lightly from time to time on cold mountain nights. I have spent nights shivering to the twinkling of the stars, and waking up with heavy frost blanketing my thin Fred Meyer "special" sleeping bag. But we lived and we learned that way. And I am a better wilderness traveler today because of those times.

A wilderness trip does not begin the first morning out in the woods. Rather, wilderness travel begins with setting priorities long ahead of time, and with serious consideration of dearly-held values. How we traverse a stretch of wild country might well set a congruous course with an inner life, feeding our daily ideals back in a country place, a hometown, or even a city street. If indeed it takes a wilderness trip to let loose and live, then could there burn a signal fire casting smoke shadows across a damaged landscape of living? We have the responsibility to find ways of living that uncomplicate, lessen distractions, and center our attention on meaning. Wilderness can remind us of value and it can reappoint meaning, but wilderness will not live our lives for us. Reflection is up to us.

Logan bread is a semi-indestructible mixture of flour, blackstrap molasses, honey, dried milk, and about whatever else you want to toss in. If I ever decide to get back into rock climbing, I first plan to make many batches of logan bread just for the exercise, for the only possible way to mix the goo is to dig in with both hands. This part of the process compares to about two dozen fingertip push-ups. But I do not make logan bread for the exercise.

I love to eat logan bread, though my family frowns on it as if it were a bad habit. Logan bread can be lunch in one big brown biscuit—just keep the water handy for swishing it down. Never mind the look of it. If you don't like molasses, hold your nose with your free hand. I mix it up with bits of dried apples or peaches, which add distinctive chewiness to the mouth-watering crusted dough. But I do not make logan bread because I love to eat it.

Baked crispy, logan bread lasts for weeks in a pack. It is hard and does not become crumbly if wedged between cookset and tent poles. Its bricklike constitution could make a mason run for a trowel. But I do not make logan bread because I appreciate its long life.

I make logan bread because it is the right thing to do. I find that in the making I enter a process consistent with journeying close to the earth. In making the bread I set a clear direction undetermined by prepackaged grocery store culinary minds. My wilderness sojourn begins in sticky batter clinging to the hairs and crevasses of my fingers and up to my wrists. As my hands dive into the mess, my mind enters the journey, and I am transported in time to a lakeside luncheon on Saganaga or Gabimichigami or Ge-be-on-e-quet. Right there in the kitchen, next to the sink and the stove, I find my spirit floating along rock ridges and ledges that drop abruptly to the rolling swells and wave crests below. I can taste the bread lifted to my lips on the updraft of campfire smoke, and I know the future satisfaction of something substantial in my belly.

But most of all, I make logan bread because it places me

fully in the act. One cannot be a sideline player and expect the logan bread to mix or shape or bake on its own. One does not find logan bread at the market, and I have no one else who will make it for me. Logan bread exacts a price from me, for it takes away my time for distractions. It calls for a simple commitment, it muddies my other choices, and it seals my traveling fate.

Rainy Nights

There are things to be learned from cold, rainy nights out in the woods. The amount of rain your tent will let in, the rate at which your sleeping bag will soak up that rain, and your talent for sleeping despite that creeping wet feeling: all these tests of appropriate gear and personal stamina are important to the wilderness traveler. Staying dry, or at least staying happy when wet, can often be the key to survival. Attitude is not the least defense against succumbing to the forces of the inclement weather.

One spring weekend about twenty years ago, I spent a cold, wet, memorable night close to timberline in the Oregon Cascades. The four of us were anticipating some great fishing from the shores of a gorgeous, shimmering mountain lake, come morning. Those were the days of tube tenting for poor folks like us who could not afford real camping equipment. A tube tent is a sheet of plastic that forms a tunnel with both ends open. You put a rope through it to hold up the top and stretch out the bottom with a few rocks. And there you have it, instant tent! If this sounds appealing, forget it, for a tube tent will only bring you grief.

Our first night out, a cold front moved in and brought with it layers of clouds prepared to unleash their salvo of water missiles. With two bodies per tube tent we settled in for the night. The rain—and my determination to hate tube tents—began before midnight. It rained hard and steadily for about five hours while I tried to stay comfortable and dry. Sure, plastic is waterproof, lightweight, and easy to pack along. But with two gigantic holes at each end and 30 square feet of floor to collect water and serve as a rain gauge, I can tell you we got soaked. The night seemed to last forever as I tried contortions Houdini would have applauded—anything to stop the total saturation of my sleeping attire. And so the first slight graying of the morning darkness provided the incentive to leave my water bed; anything was better than shivering helplessly within that plastic tube.

Though the rain continued, it at least stopped pouring. I donned my rain poncho and headed to where we had enjoyed a warm fire the night before. Instead of glowing coals, I found black puddles of ash water still filling with raindrops and oozing dark lavalike liquid down the sides of the rocks. This discovery was disconcerting; I had hoped to light a fire to bring some cheer to the morning.

There was just enough light for me to see my way among the douglas firs and the pines. After clearing the water from the fire ring, I began my search for firewood. Having arrived at our campsite late the previous evening, we had not bothered gathering and storing any dry wood. We surely had not anticipated a flood. Now I was dealing with wet wood everywhere. Whether or not this was a hopeless effort did play in my mind. But having been wet for much of the night, and still feeling cold and soggy, the thought of a warm fire was enough to send sparks of action to my waking brain.

I began by gently fingering the tiny threadlike branches of undergrowth on western red cedar and quaking aspen and shrubs like the sitka alder. Even after an extended downpour some of these have dead, dry branches because they are protected from the rain by the canopy of the trees. But it took great care and plenty of time to find any dry branches and to keep them protected from moisture. I knew that if even one raindrop landed on this tinder, I would have to begin again. So as I gathered, I tenderly stacked those minute logs tightly side by side and inside my front shirt pocket, hidden from the rain by my jacket and my rain poncho, one of the few places on my body that was dry. I still remember protecting that tinder like it was my infant child, naked and needing warmth and succulence.

Usually after a hard rain one can still find a few larger twigs and small branches of various sizes that have also been sheltered by the forest canopy. But here the woods was open enough and the rain had been so long and heavy that I met with defeat. I searched and searched, but found nothing that I could lay atop my precious tinder. Nothing, that is, until I glanced in the direction of a downed log lying partially off the ground.

The log was positioned in such a way that I could get to its underside with a hatchet, and it was big enough so that much of the interior wood was protected from the rain. That log had lain in its position for several years, judging by the rate of decay in its outer wood. How many rainstorms must it have seen since its downing, and how many neighboring trees would gain rising strength from its falling decay? Would it permit me to use its resources so that my friends and I might meet a more immediate need? My answer seemed to come in the knowledge of the many trees all about me serving the mountainside well with a plenitude of the green and fibrous living and dying cycle. The crumbs that I could gather from that log would not be missed from the table of feasting all around me.

Though I now had a source of dry wood, my job was far from easy. The rain continued its pattering beat on my head and hands, and even into my face as I looked up at the log's vulnerable underside from my kneeling position. Chipping out pieces of wood became an awkward task. Kneeling on the forest carpet of moss and grass was not lowering the moisture content in my pants. It took a vigilant gaze at the flying wood chips in order to rescue the dry ones from the well armed and aiming fire warden of the skies above.

Finally, after about an hour's concentration, I had mined deep into the heart of that old log and found the treasure I sought. As I carefully hid the dry wood chips in my pack to keep them dry, I planned my next move. The only task remaining before lighting the fire was to find some larger pieces of wood that could sustain the fire and provide hot coals for cooking a warm breakfast and cheering the soul. These could be downed wood, but not soaking on the forest floor, not green and not decayed, but with bark intact. I searched, found, and cut a supply to match my specifications. With the wood piled close to the fire ring and protected from the rain, I stripped the wet outer bark from those logs with my knife. A bit of drying heat from the fire and they would burn well.

The match held its glowing ambience. Ignition passed quickly into a small blazing radiance, and my sleepless desires unfolded into crackling flame radiating the anticipated warmth. As I lovingly placed the larger wood chips and branches atop the growing flame, I only nearly matched the growing satisfaction bred from a labored contentment bought and paid for by the hours of gathering. The warmth of the fire was no adequate measure of the radiance gained from the creative process, the single-minded searching purpose, and the lifting of the cold-hearted longing.

A unity came to birth from the simple task, and meaning caught root outside the confusion of plural purpose.

The One Thing

Stimulus quickens the mind, promotes more rapid childhood development, and provides entertainment. So why not surround ourselves with brightly-colored representations of all of life's pleasures? What about the good that comes from human creativity? All around us we can see, hear, touch, smell, and taste the variations of human thought marketed via the media. So why not cheer on this infection of consumer-driven society as it advances into the wilderness? Life is not simple you say, so why falsely alter life to accommodate a natural setting?

We are taken up, distracted, and attracted by many things, confused by our options because one question remains unanswered by stimulus. Four simple words arrest our sleep and plague our shopping sprees: *What gives meaning*? Without a living, growing, birthing, dying, and rising answer to *this* question, all our creativity may lead us further and further from our heart's quest.

In the careful preparations enlivening the weeks and months before a wilderness trip, I am drawn down the banks of the river solitaire. Suppose that my simple mind is drawn by a simple lust for freedom ringing from the halls of no carved statue of human knowledge. It truly lifts me, this singing wilderness, as Sigurd Olson once called it, into a river's moving unity, a junction of kindred performers advancing as an army opposed to voices contesting the single deep pulse of fluid in the channel. As water courses to the sea, so I ride a single rail into the land beyond human time, where God sets the clock and strikes the chime for the marriage of imagination and organic matter. God is met in simplicity.

As a raven would rasp out a call to flight, two women host the God-child for just such a holy and beckoning moment. Christ the wandering teacher has come into their home and into their presence with the reality of sacred concourse. Their dwelling, properly prepared and appointed to host God, must surely radiate true devotion. If we truly loved such a savior, would we not do all the pampering of a responsible host?

Caught in the cross fire between doing and attending, only one chose to sit and listen, perhaps touching the loosely hanging garments, whispering to herself the echoes of God's voice. Mary focused her heart on the source of joy. Martha carried forth the preparations and inevitably revealed her preoccupation with self. The distractions played as real life; the concerns gripped her from behind and overpowered her. She saw the same duties and expectations that you and I would have seen. In her judgment, these distractions embodied devotion, as lip-synching might replace a melody from the soul.

As we live, we enter this same story. We host the visit of God within every breath that we take. We make choices, wary of distractions, but lost amid the tempest of the roaring cacophony of life's demands. We have a thousand choices, a thousand doors to open and enter where Christ is not found. Some would choose the variety package that includes a taste of the generosity of wealthy doorways. Some would choose from the resources of obligation, knowing well the church teaching of the law. And some would choose doorways hewn by their own hands and call these the gates of heaven.

Martha and Mary show us the eternal test for the will of humanity. Reluctant to let go of personal choice, we always hold desperately to other options and look constantly for betterment. It is within this simple story of women's longing that dread may arise from our searching hearts. Of necessity we may look to Mary for our model, though human hearts do not want things so simple. Mary chose the only one of the thousand doorways that does not often seem to be an option. Mary chose to sit at Jesus' feet and listen to him. This choice she made is a true choice, though it is made at an ever deeper level than we may want to believe. The frightening truth is that the thousand doorways that appear to be our only options can never register on the same scale with the choice of the one. For as long as we struggle with the thousand, though righteous in our pious search for religious relevance in this world, our minds remain confused. No firm selection from among the thousand has ever ended the dissonance of decision making for very long.

The powerful theme of this woman's story leaps at us from a surprise angle with force enough to grant us hope. If indeed we are prepared to seek, the act of Mary speaks the possibility. If only Mary's choice is not too simple for us, too single-minded, and too selfless. Before the justification of another doorway, before the temptations of bright lights and fancy living, before the knee-jerk response of learned beliefs, Mary chose to place herself in God's presence. She placed herself there fully. Otherwise, the distractions would have drawn her off, just as they did Martha.

To first place ourselves, as Mary did, in God's presence, is indeed the one thing that will not be taken from us. This lives then as the single-minded act of true simplicity. Through this doorway we discover a simple world free of contrived needs and unrequited longings.

If one questions the meaning found in a simple act where attention is focused with a single purpose, then logan bread will not sustain the weary traveler. The growing warmth of reddening coals will not dry the damp of mountain mornings. And Christ's words will not bring joy to Mary.

Stuart Lake

The summer sun beat down upon us. Even in the north country July heat can be fierce. As we crossed Iron Lake, the wind had blown three-foot waves to cross our bows and toss us nearly into nausea. I pulled with all my strength on my paddle blade and watched with uneasy expectation as the other canoes danced odd reels across the water's surface. Now the wild ride was only rolling in my thoughts as perspiration covered my body, for the passage from Iron Lake to Stuart Lake is mostly by trail.

Few forest sounds are loud enough to break through one's throaty and labored breathing while portaging canoes. From the plodding of boots along the trail with occasional scuffling across rocky areas, to the small but important smack of a hand across a wet forehead to slop off the excess salt from eyebrows and furrowed temples—the body's labor drowns out all other sound. The canoe overhead echoes with this heightened awareness of the body's function. Activity—the expending of energy across the portage—claims an adjusted higher value placed with great care and targeted with pinpoint accuracy for the trophy—the trail's end.

And so the afternoon grew old as I lumbered over dead trees, angled past a dying lake, and trudged up the last hill. I prayed—almost out loud—in an attempt to rise above my painful noises. The prayer was for a gracious welcome from Stuart Lake. Since this would be our first acquaintance, and the journey here had been so costly, I feared the worst for myself and my sweat-soaked followers. For all I knew at that final incline, Stuart Lake could have been a sinkhole of turbid, weed-choked waters. This was not the planned route, but a diversion, and one which I had not checked out in advance. Stuart Lake was a risk, and we had gambled with the stakes of great labor. If we lost the hand, my friends behind might turn unforgiving faces my way.

At the top of that last hill I stopped a moment to catch my breath, my pack and my canoe balanced on my shoulders. For that brief moment I could draw from all my senses the feeling of total seclusion. I was closed in, enveloped by the forest in a place that I had never touched or smelled before. With my heart still beating hard from labor, I was caught up in an epiphany of the woodland, riveted for just an instant, the overpowering presence of luxuriant, green

life at my feet and all around. The vastness of all the forest-
ed acres captivated my mind and lodged every optic fiber
of sight within the halo in which I stood staring at nothing
more than trees, simply trees.

The moment passed as swiftly as it had come, and I
began my search for the trail's end. As the last few yards
opened to a clearing, I stumbled out into full sunshine.
Clear, fresh water and a sandy beach awaited me. As I set
my gear down I could not wait to tell the others the good
news. I ran back for them with words of encouragement,
describing a place of beauty, a place where labors would
cease and senses could indeed cast about for revelations
known only to the sacrificial travelers.

The second time I viewed Stuart Lake my friends were
with me and we stumbled out of the woods together. The
lake itself was a mirage turned into reality. It demanded the
attention of our hot and dirty bodies as we obediently
stripped to our shorts and plunged into its cold bosom. My
body prayed a thankful prayer as we thrashed about crazi-
ly, laughing off the wear of miles. Stuart Lake became a
place to sit amidst the flowing robes of divinity.

We lifted the canoes onto a low rock ledge—the lip of an
ascending rocky scale projecting fully one hundred yards
into the main body of the lake. This ledge would harbor us
for the night. The wind remained strong from the northwest,
rippling our nylon tents as we anchored them awkwardly to
the earth. Rock became our walkway between the water's
edge and campfire ring. There were many levels of stone to
explore and settle into. Gathering, hanging, storing, arrang-
ing, and resting fashioned that place into our home. You
could have called it bleak, without the sheltering of any siz-
able trees, but the variety of elevation gave it character.

Darkness found us gathered around the campfire, sitting
on logs or on the rock, searching in the black for the last of
the hot chocolate. Down to the end of the hot drink supply,

we all knew that the morning would bring us back to civilization. We did not care that the trip would end soon. We did not care that the night had drawn around us. We did not care that the wind still blew. We had entered that time of quietude when voices take on a hushed quality and people listen to other people.

I sat there, feeling the hard angle of the rock under me, smelling someone else's mosquito repellent, and watching the coals of the fire pulsate with the sucking of air. Enchantment was perhaps upon us, for tired as we were, we could not leave that circle. As I sat transfixed, I looked closely at the men seated around. Their differences took me by surprise. Some were big and strong, some were aging with white stubble poking from their jaw lines. Some were young and so slender that I thought they could break. They were talking about weakness, of all the topics to choose on a wilderness night.

They had my full attention. I listened as they spoke of their experience over the last several days. Grown men—construction workers no less—speaking of their struggle to paddle down the full length of those lakes, and of their fear of being unable to keep pace with the group. I heard them relive the portage trails and their admission of exhaustion with claims for the need of frequent rest. They marveled at the rugged beauty of that place and their own soft response to it. This indeed was unusual talk for such a group as these men, the strong and fit of our society.

As the conversation ebbed on into the night, I wandered amid my own thoughts. I had seen them work so hard and assimilate so much new experience during those days together. Just that morning we had nearly been defeated by the wind and waves on Iron Lake. And that very afternoon I had watched them toil, with heavy loads and trembling muscles, seeking their way to this place of mystery.

They talked on, listing some of their little pleasures and

laughing about the walleyes that got away, while my mind pushed on to the next morning and the route we would take to their waiting van. Our last day was to bring the toughest physical challenge yet. Stuart River, with its beaver dams and portage trails waited for us. This route ends with a 460-rod portage trail, twice as long as any trail that we had crossed during the past days. I could see them groaning under the weight, panting up the hills, slopping through the bogs. Their faces, creased with pain, looked at me hauntingly from the night.

Still the campfire conversation pushed on, now into issues of family matters: relationships and loved ones, loss and uncertainty, weakness on other fronts. Finally, I caught the significance of what was happening there. The spirit of the place had been wrapped with the shedding of layers from hardened minds. After five days of living together we were finally present to one another. We were sitting at each other's feet and listening to real words. That place had become our place and no distractions could have possibly lifted us off that rocky campsite. The wind blew through our hair, the firelight fluttered, the stirring movements of men spoke their desire to hear more, to feel more, to take in everything around them.

A bond forms when we are fully present to another person. This is the adventure of wilderness: the stripping of non-essentials from our eyes, so that our vision is not clouded or blocked or scattered. On a windswept, rocky cleft in life we huddle, almost naked, so simple, so natural to our surroundings. We see as if seeing for the very first time. But we can resist if we want; we can pack along every sort of unnecessary item; and we can hold closely to all the world from which we have come.

But that night the men in our group let go. The choice had been made, and now I know again that Mary's choice is possible.

An Unfolded Adventure

In Matthew 6 Jesus speaks in favor of the single eye—the whole body depends on it. The Greek word for *single* carries the English meaning of a sincere simplicity, a singleness of sight and mind. This concept of simplicity is used infrequently in the New Testament, but where it is used it also carries the sense of a healthy generosity. From our earlier story, Mary clearly reveals this pure and simple sight when she chooses the one thing.

Our word, *simple*, finds its roots in the Greek word *plex*, meaning fold. Thus, in straightforward usage, simplicity is the concept of being in a spread-out state, without folds ("Unfolded and Enfolded by Mercy" by Elaine Prevallet in *Weavings*, vol. V, no. 3, May/June 1990, p. 8). I liken this concept to that of a tablecloth spread out without wrinkles awaiting the table setting.

If we place the Greek and English meanings together, our understanding of the simple adventure becomes clear. We discover a dynamic metaphor for life in the unfolding process. I use unfolding in the sense that we choose not to continue being folded up into ourselves, layered no more with our ever multiplying self-desires. Instead, we are freed from the many things that would keep us from fully entering God's presence. This is the process of opening ourselves completely to God's world, for it is God's world and God's realm of activity with us. We become the tablecloth spread smoothly, prepared to accept God's china. This represents an end to all deception, where our lives become truthful again, and where distances can be crossed without the maze of self-enfolding.

Wilderness becomes a single pursuit to find an unfolded mind and a place to sit and listen. Wilderness is a wonderful place to do the theology of Mary's focused anticipation. Wilderness is the place to see the world with the simple eye, and so bring wholeness to all other aspects of our lives.

Wilderness is where we ought to spread ourselves like honey over freshly-baked bread, hot from the oven, smelling fully of life's nutrients.

But even this is not all the meaning conveyed in simplicity. Picture yourself spread out as a tablecloth, laid bare across a wooden frame, now available to receive all that God has to offer. At this moment of pure receptivity, you have become the generous benefactor, for the setting that God bestows upon your open frame is communion for the world. In both Matthew 20:15 and James 1:5 the same Greek word for *simple* is used to describe the generosity of God. When we truly achieve the posture of simplicity we become the one who receives *and* the one who gives, for there is ideally a oneness linking both acts. A generous person can give and receive, while a receptive person can receive and give.

The open, unfolded presence of mind and body enables one to gather inwardly the smells, sights, and sounds in nature. To sit under the starry canopy, to hold in memory the thoughtful notes of crying loons, to shiver the north breeze down your spine, to rub a calloused finger down shadowy tree bark, and to envision your presence in that place from the beginning of time—that is the experience of the unfolded wanderer come home at Christ's feet. To learn the wisdom of nature's words within this posture can be but a heartbeat from sitting at the feet of the One called by us the Word of God.

In like manner, this open and unfolded presence of mind and body truly offers a living sacrifice, alms for the fresh night air and promise to the cool, clear waters, peace to the forest grandeur and love for the native lives in countless form. It is a Godlike presence we embody now, surely an image to cast the bust of creation's original unfolded One. For now, in our solidarity, we have God's own goodness set upon us and spread wide for holy distribution. The communion bread and cup for the earth is set within our commitment to an unfolding, living adventure.

Simple Living

Keeping a wilderness trip simple is a challenge, especially when leading and guiding a group of people new to the experience. At the same time, it is particularly important for leaders to model simplicity. This includes streamlining what and how we pack, but it goes much further than our checklist. The simplicity described here produces a lifestyle reaching far beyond a one- or two-week canoe trip. This simplicity is the foundation for a lifelong spirituality. It potentially orders our day-to-day living, prepares our hearts for all covenant relationships, and frees us to live true and authentic lives.

Think of your many different commitments and relationships as balls. We juggle these weighted balls at speeds and in numbers beyond any realistic level. Many fall to the floor and shatter into brokenness. Ours can become a world of high-pressure stakes where the magician or clown with a flare for acrobatic display must act out the mechanistic clamor for more, more, more. Artistic, gifted play only lingers in our memory.

In our story about Mary and Martha, why did Martha fuss over the preparations in the first place? Why was a simple meal not good enough, or the house not clean enough? When the crown of life was within arms' reach, what drove her to search out other improvements? Perhaps we should ask ourselves this question: when God's robes flow about us and before us in the wonderful gifts of the earth, what drives us to search on, unsatisfied?

All our striving means little if we do not live openly receptive lives, looking up into God's eyes from the beauty around us. Doing only has meaning if it is grounded in simplicity. Grounded in simplicity, every endeavor of life may be an act of worship.

I planted a tree. It may not grow, for the Kansas heat may burn it up. I dug deeply into the hard earth. The rocklike soil may never let the tree's roots pass through and into a nourishing future. I cut back the grasses, but they may just grow again and choke the tree. I left a trench to catch the summer rains and only hope the drought will end in time to save the tree. I brought it water, but who will carry its drink when I am gone?

I planted a tree and knew it to be my own tentative way in this world. I knew it to be a good deed with all the spreading potential of lapping up sunlight. I knew myself to feel the dependency and weakness in delicate root fibers and unopened buds. I knew the fears of unanswered questions and brewing storms.

But just the same, I planted it because it sucks its sweetness from the ground and licks the yellow from the sun's own face. Its life is pure and simple. And I plant it where it can catch all the God-words whispered by the wind and echoed in the ground. Like the lilies of the field, this tree will ask no further adornments but God's own dress. And the true water, that wet miracle, will flow from the moist breath of God.

The tree will offer its shade, just as surely as it stands, opening heavenward and growing on God's behalf.

God is the shepherd of my life,
  In God's care I lack nothing.
This most loving God lays me down in green pastures,
  Leads me beside still waters,
    And restores my soul.

        Psalm 23:1-3
        author's paraphrase

Chapter 7

Healing
the
Human Spirit

The Depths of Argo Lake

Argo Lake spreads out across a pristine wilderness on the Canadian side of the Ontario-Minnesota border. You can see right through Argo Lake, as if the bowl it inhabits was intending to magnify its depths and display secrets other lakes hold private. Argo is like the osprey who plunges from a great height through the clarity of a sun-blanketed wilderness morning, diving to find its prey below the shining surface. What lives in Argo's depths is revealed, made known to the world for all its flushing envy in its transparent hues of green and blue. Argo Lake calls strongly to the canoeist above the saturation of millions of wilderness acres.

Seven heard this call and responded. We loaded the canoes quickly in anticipation of entering a vast domain of countless fresh images. We were excited as we dug our boots into the gravel shore for the last time, pushing the

117

canoe bows fully eighteen feet out onto Moose Lake. It was a shallow beginning, with many small rocks gasping for a lingering touch of the stern bottoms. Tiptoeing into cool waters with once dry boots made for hasty movement and diminished the grace of our departure. But the moment had come; we settled easily into an awareness that the adventure no longer called, but now whispered its arrival.

Deep gray clouds rolled above us, layering the sky, and moved with licking tongues to encase us in the primal journey, as if sealing us off from all retreat. Only minutes passed before we needed our rainwear. Such a morning brings with it a mystery of romance, twisted into a feeling of uneasy anticipation as the clouds and the lake water form a gamboling brew, uncertain of its mischievous outcome. And so we dipped our paddles in the brew, gladly knowing that we would chance the weather and chance the loss of society's grip.

We took a northerly aim, striking out into regions of dark water and green forest. But we also took an inward aim, striking out into less traveled country and seeking some unopened territory where living realms of mind and heart too often go unheeded. As the shorelines lengthened behind us, something within us cracked, weakening as we stroked our way into wilderness. We were friends, the seven of us, though some friendships were more newly-formed. Brought together by our desire to grow within that pure and natural setting, we chose the splendid art of faith exploration on the move through time and beauty. Thus we joined that seminar on the water, proposed to hold renewal for Christian leaders. And the weather that morning spoke to us and claimed to be holding us duty bound to the task of releasing the yoke of life.

To stroke along the side of a canoe for hours sets a tone for thought, it paces body and mind in external and undeniable routine. It can gradually twine around spirit, lashing it to the body's mast. Like a vise clamping in movement, that which is held together so tightly may form one solitary, vibrant, and coursing purpose: unity, all of a person, bound with potential. The constant breezes, bringing with them rich aromas, and the rhythmic rocking of the canoe, and the constant rollicking of the waves as they fixate the paddlers gaze: all this converts a once timid soul into a wilderness traveler.

The miles fell past our canoe bows that first day out, and we entered the vast Canadian waters of Basswood Lake. We ate lunch on a grassy perch overlooking the gray miles ahead of us. As we sank back into our canoes, we forged our way past islands that appeared and disappeared like mirages set in a London fog. The afternoon brought us dipping past Canadian Point, where we pulled in awhile to stretch our legs, eat some gorp, and study the maps for a likely campsite.

We found a small, secluded beach. It met the lake within the narrow end of a cove, and it boasted a small level area amid tree roots. There would be enough space if we crowded our three tents close together. The forest towered over us in that small place. A near mountain of boulders upturned the forest floor in a steep ascent but ten paces from the sand. We were cupped in a cubbyhole of misty intrigue, left there to forage for our thinking in the evening of that day. And as we thought through our impressions of the vast land we had entered, we eased into the work of creating a place of shelter from the elements. We scattered into the tasks with renewed energy, as our minds settled on the thought of the hot coffee and tea soon to steep in pots over the fire.

Wind bore in on us, even past the supper hour when we lounged lazily about the fire area. We appreciated the rain tarp for its protection from the big drops of water blowing off the treetops above us. Not long after supper, the blazing rays of the sun streaked into our forest home. Those clouds that had marched above the fullness of the day now parted awhile. After the long day of half light, our eyes were forced to blink and wince in the brilliance. The sun's rays were a sign of good weather to come, a trusting glimmer of the next morning, and a signal flare to cap off the waning daylight and secure the last of our tired satisfaction.

That night, seated on the sand at the water's edge, we gathered our thoughts and began our daily journey of release. We were learning to let go of the hierarchical thinking that places a price tag on life forms and things of nature. In doing so, we began a process of personal transformation from closed to open, from taskmaster to servant, from foreigner to friend. This letting go claims a new place for us within creation, a place without the hatred and condescending inherent in hierarchy. Letting go has great significance for relationships between humans and all varieties of creatures. But this night we focused on ourselves. We asked, "What does this release mean for a person's spiritual health?" To take those thoughts and the accompanying questions seriously begins to unravel the cords that have us humans tied up within ourselves.

That first night out, the unraveling began for each of us. It was perhaps in the tenor of our voices or in the silence that followed speech, that the releasing caught a foothold and wedged in our thoughtfulness. Of course, the romance of that place, wedged in time and space, aided the spell that bound us to the unfolding. Though at that time we could not have known it, the die was cast; the trip would take us unexpectedly to protected regions that harbored deep feelings. We closed that day with prayer for the courage to follow the inner path now set for us.

As the days passed, we celebrated life in a hundred ways. From the breathtaking waterfalls, to the wild ride of the rapids, to the total silence of the heart as we rested—motionless—on a solitary shore, we thrilled at the joys of living in wilderness and we laughed ourselves silly, enjoying each other's company. The eggshells surrounding each of us waited to crack, like small dams waiting the right moment to burst.

Our fourth day out we searched out portages and skimmed across half a dozen small lakes. We listened to an occasional loon call and the plop of painted turtles as they escaped our presence. A few of the lakes were shallow and especially dark-bodied, with a fullness of sediment and marsh stain. In that still water, tadpoles played wiggling games of tag, while the fragrant white water lilies rode high and majestic above the surface. We passed through the environs of wedge-leaved arrowhead, marsh spike rush, three-way sedge, and nodding beggar-ticks. From a distance a blue jay gave its harsh cry, and along the water's edge a belted kingfisher imitated white-capped wave action in its flight. The day was balmy as the sun rode high above the moderate breeze, and we pulled our hat brims down low to save our sight. The portage from Cone Lake became a killer in the heat and uphill climbing, but Argo Lake shone as a beacon from the west, guiding us onward.

We eased onto Argo's near perfect glaze, for the wind was behind us and twisted within the treetops, held by the baffling of pine and fir needles. Stretching out before us as a wildflower prairie would entice hungry deer at evening, we felt the refreshment reflect off the mirror-like surface. We barged the canoes for lunch. Adrift on the lake, we fared well, like banqueting sailors courting the love of a Tahitian lagoon and the gratitude of native cuisine. Our work had ended while the sun stood tall in the sky. In praise for natural elements of the northwoods, we studied our surroundings and collected our plans for our lodging on Argo Lake.

Exploring the third campsite brought us to a sheltered north bay with granite layers of ship-sized rocks. Thick stands of wild blueberries, low and pregnant with fruit, stretched out before us. The clear water dropped abruptly off the edge of the granite, and so it was a swimmer's haven. From atop the rock, the lake spread south. It was a spectacular scene. Nothing could have greeted us with greater honor; the welcome overran the pitcher's capacity to pour.

After camp was set up, the remainder of the day became a frolic of swimming, fishing, and gorging on wild blueberries. The sun was already low when we ate a late supper. All the while we stole glances around us and mentally pinched ourselves to see if we were really there in that garden. The pulse of our lives had suddenly changed, for we planned to lay over the next day to fully enjoy all that Argo Lake had to offer. Instead of packing tents and stuffing sleeping bags in the morning, we would lounge in primitive style throughout the entire day. That thought alone was enough to fill us with eager anticipation.

We ended that fourth day seated by the lake, looking south over the waters under the dying light. Our sharing turned to a discussion of life's essentials. What is the significance of human life within the universe? Where do we belong? What is important about our lives? Is it not essential to acknowledge that we exist as but a molecule of the universe, and then take that thought and wrestle it to the ground and look it in the face? Was Carol P. Christ correct when she wrote that this is essential religious insight (*Weaving the Visions*, ed. Judith Plaskow, Harper Collins, 1989, p. 321)? Might this be what it means to recognize God in our praises to divine glory as shown to us by this world? And then what is left to us? What is left for this small human substance of body, soul, and brain?

While these questions can sometimes lead into useless mind games, that night—with the rock and water and low light surrounding us amid the spell of wild country—these questions signaled a solid search of our spirits. Thought, rooted in living experience as concrete as boulders and the body and blood of dear friends, had the chance to expand into reality.

We slept that night, dreaming. The thin mossy cushion between the rock bed and our sleeping bodies could have told the story of darkly moving figures, restless before the power of those dreams. Was it the cool night air blowing down from the pine tops and in through our tent windows that brought those dreams? Or did they rise from tears of the human spirit? Could the forest creatures have sensed our needful hearts? Or could the rhythm of the stars overhead have forced a gravitational release, as inevitable as a mountainside avalanche?

Some say that our dreams reflect our subconscious; that they are a type of veiled, yet unconfined, expression. Dawn brings the recession of the dark's freedom images, but may still tenderly hold the truth revealed just under the heart's surface.

The yellow day was sounded by the rustling of small birds, as sleep-logged eyes rolled skyward. It was a slow morning, full of time and warmth and our renewed amazement at Argo Lake's infectious charm. Once again the spell of the wild sought us and we could not cower or hide, though we still pretended not to be fully taken in and owned by what seemed a benign presence. After all, is not nature a neutral, though useful, tool of the human hand? Is it not simply our helpmate as we build a better society? Such a thought might have ended our inner voyage long before we left the woods.

By mid-morning we all gathered together, just out of reach of the blueberry patch, wanting to collect our thoughts rather than the delightful fruit. The large rock was already warming from the bright yellow touch of the sun. We sat close, gazing again into Argo's depths. It was T-shirt weather that day. The removal of our jackets was perhaps the signal of something more. In such a potentially harsh environment, we had learned another lesson in trust and vulnerability. Even the heights of summer can bear the hardships of winter storms, and the bright light can always return to cold gray. But in that moment, we felt that all the north country at one command had joined ranks for a cease-fire worthy of total relaxation and endurance beyond all our needs.

Gathered there, we turned our attention to words of healing as Perry became our teacher. He spoke of Job and God and the meaning of God-with-us. He spoke of personal pain laid beside the biblical story, and he sought to encourage us to deal honestly with the perplexities of tragedy and divine benevolence. There must be no easy answer, for an easy answer hides the pain and cheats us of our deeper living.

Following Perry's words, we rose in silence to an extended time of personal reflection. And as we each sought our own space along Argo's banks, one whose pain had surfaced overwhelmingly—one whose inner dam had broken fully—remained on that warm gathering site, weeping tears as long as Job's. Her heart broke open to the sun and the water; the very pores of the rock received the giving of her sorrow. And Perry caringly shared her solitary walk through life's dying within the face of that morning. And when one's inner holding fails to stop the floodwaters, the surface cracks of others' shells may widen beyond the help of even emergency sealants.

As our friend opened her heart, unable to hold back its feelings, we each swallowed hard as our own emotions took us into the morning air with an urgency. I sought a small, grassy plot where our campsite leveled for a moment before arching sharply toward a fifteen foot fall to the lake. I found that I could not pull myself out of earshot of the weeping. I was held by my own need to meet with the engineer who had dammed up my insides, and that engineer looked very much to be me. The weeping I heard grew louder and closer to my own heart, and I began to hear myself, and to feel the salt tears scald my own cheeks. Suddenly the trip into wilderness became more than I had bargained for. I struggled to keep my image of leadership, if only to impress myself.

During those next two hours of silence, I must have cried a dozen times. And still I was holding back, telling myself that the release was good and just what I needed. But I clutched an even deeper need that I did not allow to be tapped, for the fire danger was too high, and the flame might burn out of control. Yet each time the tears subsided I felt relief and a sense of loosening of the burdens on my back. Little by little, my load was lightening.

I ended my silent time there on that patch of green by leaping into a dive. I mirrored the shape of the stone arch as I moved through the air and plunged deep within the blue water below. The cold shock on all my skin created a silent scream that was unleashed into eight feet of water. But for the cold, I could have mistaken Argo for my mother's womb, as my mind rejoiced in the safety of the fluid embrace.

We gathered for lunch without speaking, for we were all still emerging from our inner journeys. The morning reflection and silent focus had shaped us all according to the dictates of outer beauty and inner turmoil. But it wasn't long before the infectious lure of wilderness adventures and playfulness caught us up for the afternoon. And with all the activity, I almost forgot the deep pressure that was still in my soul, still haunting me.

After a late supper, we gathered once again in the lengthening light down by the lake. Once again, the lake spread out before us to the south for miles, its waves gaining crests of gold from the aging sun. It was my turn to lead the group and explore further the topic of healing. I raised the issue of nature as healer, of nature as a changing and vulnerable host to the human sojourn, of nature as example of arms open in love, and of nature as arms folded in writhing pain. In our discussion I pushed for the recognition that our painful thoughts and sorrowing pasts must be taken to a deeper level where spiritual growth takes its root. I ended my sharing with the words of a prayer by Miriam Therese Winter from *Woman Prayer Woman Song* (Meyer Stone Books, 1987, pp. 160-61). The prayer ends with these two stanzas:

I believe in a God whose spirit survives
all forms of degradation,
who mediates hope that rises above the limits
of time and place
who is durable and vulnerable,
who sometimes shows a masculine mood,
more often a feminine face.

I believe in a God who holds us all
In Her everlasting arms,
Who gathers us protectively
to the shelter of Her wings,
who binds our wounds, dries our tears,
and promises better things.

After an hour of sharing closed by that prayer, our little group stayed together, searching for words to hear and to speak for the cause of honesty, and the willful release of deep emotion. But I could not stay. All through the hour there on that shore, even as I led the discussion, I fought the true meaning of our words. Finally, at the close of that hour, my own personal dam was bursting, and this time I could not hold it back. So I excused myself as my eyes swelled and my voice choked.

Quickly I moved along the shoreline and into the woods,

away from all prying eyes. Groping in the faint light, I stepped over moss-covered tree roots and dodged the branches aimed at my face. All the while, my heart was emptying the load it could carry no longer. I felt the convulsions rush from deep down. My body seemed to contract in repeated spasms. The trees themselves seemed to spread their garments around me as the dusky air moved with me through their enveloping reach.

I cried tears that had been pooling behind a shell of opaque glass for two years. Those waters were like a womb's protective fluid in full flow to herald the birthing process. My cheeks burned red-hot from traces of fiery drops that could have ignited a forest fire. Half blinded, I continued stumbling into what seemed an endless sea of tortured feelings that stabbed me again and again on their way out of my heart. Faces, many faces rose from my darkness and looked steel-like into my salt-stained eyes on their way out of me and past me. Marching, they went away from me into the night, taking away their pain. Hearing their haunting voices choked me, and I thought I might give up breathing altogether. But an unconscious will to live drove the gasps for air between my sobbing. The voices were many, but once they spoke, they faded and then died away. No longer could they be heard over my own hushed weeping.

As I rounded a small bay, a huge shoulder of rock loomed over me, gathering shadows to cast into the water far below at its feet. Though I could not fly, I fixed my wounded sights on the eagle's lair, and I climbed through the forest so that I might light upon the rock's crest. Focusing on the ascent, my clutch on emotions momentarily stabilized. I came to the top, searching for that place where I could rest between my birth pangs. Along the eastern edge of the rock's high lookout, I discovered a small cradle carved into the rock, sized perfectly for me.

Safety, protection, warming, and healing took place there during the next hour. I had many more tears to shed; the pores of the rock lapped them up willingly. Two years of walking in other's sorrow and watching as friends became enemies to one another, two years of tasting the tears of people dear to me while burying my own, two years of seeking resolution and healing for loved ones who would not face the pain of healing, two years of feeling the agony of grabbing hands tearing at me from opposite directions leaving my wounds naked. I covered them, but I could not clothe them. I had been blinded to my own spirit's depth, the way that pushing pain down only digs one into it deeper and deeper.

The rock felt solid and I named people by name, people who I never wanted to lose. Even as I named them, I knew that my world had changed. Though the two years were over now and I could sigh the longest sigh of my life, I also fully faced the thought of never going back. Beloved friends who had ministered to me were now lost to me, and the circumstances that stepped in between us had never been within my control. And so, in full darkness now, lonely prayers went up from that rock and resounded from the depths of Argo Lake. The dead calm of night in an ancient land accepted the resentment over my loss, and I said my good-byes.

Deep shadows surrounded me as a screech owl called for all the light to lie still until morning. Rapid wing beats whistled over me as two loons searched for the quiet of the lake and their watery beds. A mouse ran in spurts next to me across the rock, smelling as it went for wind-borne seeds caught in the flakes of lichen and moss. The night came alive as I rubbed the sleep of the mourner out of my eyes. As I sat up, it was like a resurrection from death, with freshness filling the air of the now empty tomb. That eagle's lair had witnessed the broken shell of my interior man now come of age. Into the living yoke burst upon dark life, I put my hope. I felt fragile, like a downy chick unfit to fly and hardly fit to walk on wobbly legs.

Timidly, I returned to camp, knowing that I would have to reintroduce myself to the others. We celebrated the healing of the day as the hour grew late and the footwork of the northern lights whirled us about the dance floor.

Well past midnight I slipped into my sleeping bag and pretended that my new body needed rest. I felt too light-headed and silly to become sober enough for real sleep, for I had closed a chapter in my life that night. I had ended those words of burden, and I had been touched by a new and cheerful God.

Expressions of a Natural Piety

God touches us in many ways. We may feel the thumb of God pressing us down and pressuring our submission into crates of cargo bound for heaven. We may joke about a God who looks like a white man on some ivory throne floating above the galaxies but requiring homage all the same. Or we may take our discipleship motif, bury our heads in the sand of obedience, and wish for that day when God will finally release us from earth's toil.

After all, life is hard work, plain and simple. What does the Lord require? Micah 6:8 says, "To do justice, love mercy, and walk humbly with your God." Jesus says in Luke 9:23 that we must deny ourselves and take up our cross and follow him. Jesus blesses the persecuted and those who mourn in Matthew 5. And seemingly, we are taught to endure all hardships of life and we even come to think of these hardships as spiritual cleansing, as winnowing out the chaff of human sin. All this we know and repeat in church services. But for many of us caught in the theology of self-sacrifice, our greatest sin may be the very attitude we employ for our salvation.

Imagine the Christian life sustained by the motif of hard work. To be tired and worn out means spiritual fulfillment. To do justice within a world where one's life work makes but a microscopic dent means continual defeat declared as triumph. To carry on the tasks that smooth the operation of congregational life spells the word duty in letters written across our foreheads for all to read. And there in that life of burden the church performs all bodily functions but exhibits no vital signs, no life.

The very same desires that drive the salvation search kill the spirit long before a real deliverance could open a closed casket. Here Parker Palmer's helpful description of the active life becomes a caricature, active but hollow of all life.

We also have what I call the abundant life motif. This is a theology of God as the "Sugar Daddy," with the emphasis on sugar, not gender. Imagine the Christian life sustained by this vision. Problems multiply in quantum leaps from televangelist sermons on giving to receive, to the utter personalization of faith. The Christian does not ask questions; we are not accountable, we just want to praise the Lord. "'Tis so sweet to trust in Jesus, just to take him at his word," as the song goes. We bless, baptize, marry, and forever eulogize that sweet addiction to Jesus like a love. This is a false simplicity, because those Christians caught in this casket wish the world would go away with all its ugly problems.

The motifs described above are two of the dominant streams of Christian life that have plagued the church for many, many years. You may describe them differently; there may be hundreds of variations and spin-offs. With them may go many forms of denial, but the church is still caught in the argument between grace and works. And the church will be caught in this argument forever if we do not stop idolizing the human place in creation. Neither side—and no combination of the two—can get us out of the struggle to see ourselves as God's chosen children. We either want to work our way into God's grace or praise our way into it.

I find no healing of my spirit in driven work or blind praise. We must have a new vision, a new paradigm that transcends the problems of cheap grace and the righteousness of works. This new vision must transform us simultaneously. For if we cannot get out of old dichotomies, then there is no hope for spiritual wholeness. If we have learned anything from our tedious religious strivings, we should have learned that they cannot give real life. Neither side has ever had the last word on producing spiritual wholeness.

I vote that we step out of these arguments altogether and express together a natural piety that takes the world around us as field for theological nurture and change. It is well past time to seek release from the imprisonment of the human struggle to embrace God. While theologians from either side of the grace and works dilemma will tell us that their theories embrace far more than human struggle, what we see from those who sit in the pews on Sunday morning speaks otherwise. There is a fundamental flaw in any theology that fails to account for the overwhelming presence of God in our world apart from, but potentially in participation and relation with, the human-God connection. There has been minimal serious theology done without this flaw during modern times. Exceptions include some feminist theology and some creation theology. If I could be proven wrong on this point, I would rejoice.

We are a needy people. We need to live within the nurture of loving relationships. This is natural and good, for this loving explains much of our reason for having been created. This loving even describes our Creator. So why have we failed to see all the potential love around us? Why have we lived in a "hostile" world? Why have we portrayed our walk with God as if God's handiwork could have no affect on our spirit? Bless the theologian's heart who seeks God in mind and spirit, but let us all cry together that this is not enough. God cannot be contained within the human experience and God will not be known as peripheral outside the human domain. Any attempt to understand God can potentially lead to a human demigod that falls far short of the real thing. Let us admit our limits of understanding, and step out of old strongholds that lead us to battle with words, useless words.

Beyond the search for God's embrace in works or grace, we might claim less knowledge and more understanding. Understanding could relax our hold on life and help us to give it up altogether. For in every person there is a dam about to burst. For most of us, the dam is major and kept sealed by piety—religious fervor chained to a post like dogs in the night. We move within the community of the church as ghosts, because we cannot seem to unchain ourselves and become real—too much water might wash through the dam and its hold on our life might be severely weakened.

Powerful hope, sustaining love, exquisite beauty, and vast spiritual healing all wait for us in urgency. While we remain over-focused on the human quest for the Divine, relationships of every shade within the color spectrum paint the world about us in God's bold hand. Now, before the world is destroyed, we must learn that theology cannot be done except within relationship. And, it is the spiritual healing of relationship which in turn produces a living theology, unlocked, caskets open, and the dead raised to life. Awakening before us is the real piety of the pews with the diversity of the soil and the multitude of living things infusing life into worship.

To view life around us as God's activity and to find spiritual joy in the love given to us by animate and inanimate friends requires a transformation of the human understanding of God. This does not mean that we get good feelings from being in nature, or that nature serves us in some way as a tool for enriching human life. Rather, this natural piety proclaims that the human soul thirsts to participate with water, trees, birds, and fresh air. Natural piety understands that we are not whole without the suckle of the land, and that there is joy to be found in animal life. Healing of the human spirit will not happen outside of God's covenant, outside our place of belonging, which leaves us actually dependent on nature's care for us. Interesting, is it not? We have always known about our dependency on nature, but most Christians removed this understanding from theology and spirituality long ago.

Yet a natural piety asks to breathe into our search for God, whatever the path we trod. Justice and peacemaking are the arms and legs of righteousness, but the worker must find healing for wounds dealt by the global strife of humanity. God's creation forms an essential framework of community where spiritual healing is the most natural art. And it is the great gift of this community to send the worker out in loving passion integrated into every act. Every effort to find God or to be justified before God is wasted effort, because being in God's embrace happens naturally. While in this natural sphere of divine composition, we ingest a love from God, and a compassion showered upon us—as in the strength of a mountain or the shoulder of the rock edged by the waters of Argo Lake. There is no more drive to work for God because God is fused to our very existence. A truly natural piety lives the work of God, breathing love in and out.

The abundant life can mean so many things. But where it looks away from the problems and injustices of life, where it seeks Jesus-love as an escape, and where it means comfort: there will be no real healing. How can true healing happen when so many relationships are trivialized and when even Divinity is seen as a personal lover? Here, praise to God too easily weds with personal need or personal ambition or personal confirmation. Once again, the healing of a natural piety must freshen the air and open a person to all of life. No praise to God can carry authenticity without the love born in relationship. No praise to God will travel beyond self if not grounded in a passion for God and God's creation.

A natural piety offers healing solace to souls caught up in cheap grace, for a natural piety places us fully in relationship. A great healing lurks within the requirements of this compassionate exchange. The person who flees the obligations of justice most certainly lacks compassion, not just for others and the world, but the compassion that could actually reside in their own soul. To be loved and to love must be the most basic divine gift to humanity, and this must be what holds the very bowels of the earth together. This loving abides as an exchange: we can love from the context of knowing we are loved. The seekers of cheap grace actually flee the empty vessels of their hearts, vessels that were always intended to overflow with love. But now we must acknowledge that there is no place in this world where we can flee the hand of God, or the embrace of God, or the caress of God's love. For God has placed us here, right here in the middle of trees and water, meadows and mountains, all teaming with life. And if that is not love and love's expression seeking vessels to fill, then our God has been a mirage and our story of faith a lie.

Our journey into the depths of Argo Lake speaks the truth and claims the one God. For anyone taking that journey, all sights, sounds, and smells bombard mind, body, and even the soul with an evangelical witness to God's immanence, at once both tender and overwhelming. This chapter speaks of healing within nature, but it does not come easily or simplistically. Even in the most ideal settings, the core of our resistance and our notions of human superiority, the terror found in our doubts and our locking control over emotions, and our prepackaged theology all scream internally that the dam must not suffer any serious impairment.

We all carry great pain; we all stand in need of great release. The greatest healing of all is that which introduces us to acceptance and love, that which offers us true friends, that which provides a community based on trust and honest disclosure. That was the real depth of Argo Lake sought and found by the seven friends. That was the experience of wilderness my own heart craved, and yet resisted, until moment by moment, hour by hour, and day by day, my ability to hold back ebbed away. Finally, all my defenses failed against the healing power of that earth beauty, the open arms of my canoe partners, and God's charming grace, flowing from it all.

Perhaps you have never before heard of a natural piety, or of creation's way past the dilemma of justified living or comfortable praise. You may have never visited a place like Argo Lake or searched the forest through blinding tears. If not, here is your invitation to spiritual healing.

Running

While running a few days ago, I turned a corner around our square country mile that brought me parallel and tight against a wooded creek bottom. It took a winter day, with all the open spaces left by fallen leaves, to show me the shades of tan and the browns of a bank cut for hundreds of years by the water. Finishing the turn and easing into the grade of a Kansas hill, I was caught off guard by a sudden crush of undergrowth at the bottom of the fifteen-foot drop to my right. Three whitetail deer, flushed from among the lower trees, dashed zigzag up the bank, racing me as they climbed.

Just as suddenly they drew me up in their gait, and for two seconds—plenty of time to think—I dashed with them. But once they reached the top of the bank they were gone, white tails swishing like feather-duster metronomes keeping time with my pounding heart. For all my want, I could not pace with them.

For two seconds I felt a part of them and I know I could have enjoyed their wild company further had they lingered. Perhaps it is just an idyllic fantasy, but I still believe that all God's creation was formed to establish community. Largely by choice, humans find themselves alienated from this community. But it is not God's will, nor must it be our will, to rub a festering wound and deny the healing of spirit.

Even now my mind races against the flanks of those deer, while my spirit soars even higher since receiving the weightless gift of my crumbled inner barriers.

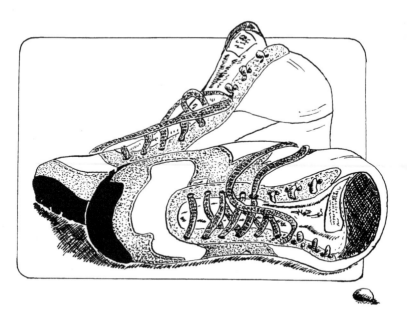

You know that among the Gentiles those whom they recognize
    as their rulers lord it over them,
And their great ones are tyrants over them.

But it is not so among you.
But whoever wishes to become great among you
    must be your servant,
And whoever wishes to be first among you
    must be slave of all.
For the 'Son of Man' came not to be served
    but to serve.

And to give his life a ransom for many.

Mark 10:42-45
author's paraphrase

Chapter 8

Servants of Natural Life

The Rub

On a gray summer morning, with temperatures down nearly to freezing, bodies move tentatively around the campsite. Muscles contract uncontrollably while brain waves ponder the meaning of past warmth. The lake water appears frozen, but it is only resting, having the sense to wait for warmth from the sun to move it into waves. Like a snapshot taken in secret, the soil and root, rock and leaf reveal details of freshness brought on by the night's cold spell. My moccasins turn a dark, blackish red from stain of dew licked off blades of grass and sponged from the coarse skin of granite that is still sleeping. I cannot remember this much new photography from my other life, yesterday. Details seem to impress me more before the sun strikes them, scattering the shadows once marking their distinctive lines. This is the atmosphere of dawn and it pervades my dream walk through the morning air.

A dying birch leaf clings flat to the leather top of my right moccasin. A similar leaf droops low at shoulder height, curved downward and waiting to release a crystal drop of dew. The oval-shaped droplet, having soothed the leaf's sides, now waits for its dive to the earth as it dangles necklace fashion off the tip of green. Night's loss and morning's gain are caught within that tiny bubble, caught and displayed for me to see like a mirror to the world. Or could it be the other way around? Perhaps the morning has confused me into thinking that I could be the reflection of the droplet's beauty.

I huddle for a time, facing west across Agnes Lake. I do not know that the low-lying, reed-filled bay just to my left will shelter a feeding moose before we break camp. Only later the delighted surprise will frame our mouths as we view the black matted hair and pumping legs surging through the shallows. The split-second glistening of black eyes and the ripple of layered muscle would only increase my sense of specific purpose in the play of nature's day. But for now, the bay is quiet and vacant. I study the changing colors of the trees on the far shore. Green is not very green—if you think about it—compared to when it brightens and shines with a morning star on the top branch. It is the sun's doing, that Christmas star giver, so I know that somewhere over my shoulder there is a golden globe searching for me, just as it has brightened the far shore.

Sitting a few seconds more in order to set my attitudinal compass for the day ahead, I feel a blunt pain from sitting on the hard rock. It calls to me, this pain, with a special rub from my right half, the location of my right hip pocket. My hip pocket packs an assortment of human mementos gained from traveling a wild environment. Here within the crowning splendor, I collected cigarette butts, wire twist ties, scraps of foil, and candy wrappers. In almost every campsite the careful archaeologist discovers a veritable mini-garbage dump, mounds perhaps like Megiddo and Babylon. And I connive to increase the difficulty and lessen the finds for future digs. Why should other centuries know our litter? Why should *this* century know our litter?

I am struck by the contrast of living things with matter that will not return to the earth, things that will not accept the hungry tummies of bacteria and other micro-organisms. These new compounds, born of our chemistry labs, mark our human trail through the woods like footprints on a newly-waxed kitchen floor. There is stench in the droppings of candy wrappers and cigarette butts.

A few years ago in September, a female black bear attempted to feed on campers who were enjoying the islands of Lac La Croix. As the local newspaper chronicled the story, the bear first attacked a lone camper on an island where the camper had been left for a solo adventure by Outward Bound instructors. Fortunately for the camper, the instructors heard his screaming as the bear dragged him into the woods by his head. They quickly returned in time to beat the bear off with their canoe paddles and save the life of the camper. Two days later the same bear attacked another camper, who was again saved when his canoe partner pounded the bear with a canoe paddle. This particular "problem" bear was soon shot by Forest Service personnel in order to make the world safe for campers (and the tourist industry).

The bear was starving at her most crucial time of the year—as she was preparing for hibernation. The ensuing autopsy showed in graphic style the contents of her stomach. Along with some human hair, compliments of one of the campers, she was plugged up with fifty pieces of black, gray, and clear plastic; two plastic produce bags; an instant soup plastic wrapper; and twenty-nine butterscotch candy wrappers. All this she attained via the unsuspecting generosity of, yes, campers. And so I ask you, was the bear the problem or the victim? Your answer to that question may show the degree to which your lifestyle depends on the supply and demand of things that aren't biodegradable. Plus, your opinion might be tainted by your territorial nature. Is the natural landscape the right of the species with greatest technological power? Does it come as a surprise to us that other species may be territorial too? To a creature that normally eats berries and insects, the invasion of the human supermarket may wield more firepower than the barrel of a gun.

My oversized wallet of "human remains" was quite literally a "pain in the butt." Sitting on a log around a campfire can yield even more pain than sitting on a rock, since the curvature of the log and the pocket's belly meet so directly in opposing form. Yet I keep refilling my right hip pocket with trash whenever I travel canoe country. And this may only make sense within the verses of a song from the musical, *Godspell*. The singer tells of a pebble placed in his shoe. The intended discomfort prods the mind away from comfort and haunts the soul with stubborn resistance. The pebble's task is to keep the human spirit honest, to not allow a memory lapse convenient for spiritual decay and personal retreat. The pebble stands for life beyond self-interest.

The only possible spiritual walk rubs against disposable journeys, for spirituality is the one truly sustainable detail of every early morning. Our material world changes form but also remains constantly organic as a sign of its connection to God and as a constant symbol of God's promise of land to Israel. But land was never promised for the purpose of ingesting plastic garbage. The bear lies still now. Its headstone should read, "No Pebbles in Our Shoes."

To Prairie Portage

Waves have various origins. Winds that blow as a result of earth's surface warming are like giant fans plugged into the sun's outlet. The resulting waves roughen the skin of lakes like sandpaper fingers from the sky. Fish that rise at dusk heave the water heavenward and penetrate its airtight seal, creating silhouetted rings of water in the moonlight. Water birds rise and fall against their liquid perch, and their energy first pulses and then drifts in lessening crests beyond the impact or thrust. Gravity pulls at waves' under-bellies along graveled creek bottoms and the entrances to lakes. Here water moves as a force to reckon with. Water bugs touch the surface with their legs—so lightweight, and they spring in horizontal leaps that rock the sleep of even the most sedate protozoa.

And so waves are the markers for travel, the sign of something passing, the water's way of giving and receiving, and yes, even the gift of resistance. This is a rub of another sort. About seven miles of uninterrupted water pave the route to Prairie Portage. This water highway is traveled by thousands of people annually. People too must find their legs for springing across this surface. For those entering the Boundary Waters wilderness from near Ely, Minnesota, Prairie Portage is the location of Canadian Customs, the Canadian Forestry Service, and a step-off into the Quetico Park wilderness of Ontario. The popularity of wilderness water here speaks for itself as the parade of boats up and down this highway never seems to end. Though a designated wilderness area stretching across three large lakes, the summer months hold little wilderness solitude here. For this pathway becomes a necessary crossing to grant the procurement of solitude and it also levels a diminishing effect on the Boundary Waters area, at least during the months free of ice.

People travel the wilderness highway to Prairie Portage inside boats invented to counterbalance our physical limitations. We swim slowly and poorly compared to other creatures. So perhaps we have boats to whisk us on our way and part the waters of impatience. For many centuries now, the canoe has been the craft of choice for wilderness adventures in this area. The canoe seems natural because of its design and versatility. Humans handle it well, and it carries the sense of becoming a part of us, a part of our personal story in time. Canoes part the water, creating low waves to forty-five degree angles on either side of the boat, while also leaving a trail of churning swirls directly behind. Water displacement is kept to a minimum, labor in the paddling is eased, and the traveling event remains unobtrusive: this constitutes a gentle leap across the water. Call it a romantic notion, but I think I actually love canoes. These boats have lured me out onto the Sea of Galilee, another fear-stained water walker to add to Christ's collection.

Perhaps one-half of the summer boats crossing to Prairie Portage are motorboats, fast and full of precision tools wed to combustion. These larger wave-makers carry more people, more goods—even canoes are flipped and held overhead by iron bars. I have always thought that an overturned canoe made an unhappy face. But the motorboat is a symbol of progress, perhaps a higher evolution, an increase in the happiness of human living, a grace for the weary or the less physically able. The motorboat provides the ride into a wilderness heart without the kindness of first words, without the romance of courtship.

Motorboats pretend to fly over the surface on their way to Prairie Portage, but all honesty must spill from the parted waters. Large waves that show the true rub dash against the shore and uncoil across the trailing scene. And whatever great energy passes the slow-growing forest edges, it cannot boast of biceps and sweat. You see, there is no self-sacrifice required on the part of humans when waters are parted by whirling props. All the rub is felt by the tool, or the ground opened in search of fossil fuels, or the birds that fly in blue-tinted air, and even the lake itself as vibrations of sound fly through sky and water alike.

As I paddle my canoe I have always watched and wondered after the boat people swirling past me with glances of mild curiosity, occasionally an upheld hand of greeting. I have always treasured the wilderness as a place where I could be cured of my impatience, my drive to move quickly, my temptation to buy improved technology. And I have never understood the reasons for speed and noise and smell beyond the human ability. Sure, I know of the desire to leap to the favorite fishing hole. I know all about the dream of procurement without effort. I know too well the mind's resistance to physical labor—a price too great for some to pay. I also know of the way that our society and culture have bred us into dinosaurs that have and take. Ours is the world of the individual who finds loneliness an isolation to be bought off, or emptiness an anger to rage against. Everything that I have is what I deserve. I justify my life a million times before I think about the outcome. I am born into this dream and it is named justification, self-justification. I am my own stronghold of freedom, my own act of liberty, my own guarantee of equal rights. I may burst upon wilderness because it is there.

I know about these undercurrents of the Western mind, yet I find that I cannot understand them anymore. The death of the female black bear has drawn me into a graveyard where the stones publish the news about pebbles grinding.

And because of all this, I am doubtful of human activity that professes a love for wild country while living society's birthright. I confess to my simplicity, for I cannot comprehend a love that does not overflow with life-giving liquid kisses. Perhaps wilderness has crippled my mind, for I seem to limp along into it while others thrust past me and court at higher tempos and speeds. Waves have various origins.

Snow in the Rockies

A few days ago I shuffled my way up a long gentle slope of snow that enveloped the mountains like a thickening blanket. Two of us were angling toward Raspberry Mountain. We moved along, mostly in silence. We were as deep in thought as the snow about us. At times our cross-country skis searched tentatively for a firm base. At times those same skis sank below the surface of snow into an unknown depth and were lost to us. It had been two weeks since that trail had last been broken, and the lengthening winter winds and additional snows had all but obliterated the passage. A corridor of pine and spruce half protected the packed trail.

The day matched my mood perfectly, for it was gray and the clouds were intermittently shadowing dark gray. Swirling snowflakes added a coat of white to my blue pile jacket. In that wind and snow I gave thanks for the uphill work that kept me warm despite the lap of winter enclosing our ascent. I was once more amazed at my reaction to the snow. The snowfall convinced me that I was entering a shadow land of mystery void of the customary shadows. Instead of dark to shade the shapes of trees and rocks, white fell all around, and I could not resist the glee of entering further into the mystery of the white shadow. The gift of the snow underfoot and all around drew me up the ascent of my inner passage, my emotional mix of knee-deep thinking.

My inner mountainside stood layered and sloping with the thoughts of others, thoughts that led away from the snowfall and the pathway up which we labored so intimately. Somehow the emotional climb and the physical climb seemed congruent. Both were necessary waters for me to part; they were my leap across the surface of "Christian" thinking. For once again the lines from some holy play had been quoted to me. The words of some artful wisher echoed too loudly through the centuries. And the wishing and the acting bore the marks of angels' wings flying about the earth's surface, therefore carrying the soul away from the rub of an earthly dream. More plainly, the vocabulary of dreams spoken to me that day quoted the sanctity of the eternal human soul over against any present urge to heal the earth and the earth's creatures.

We had just finished a weekend of teaching Bible and environmental responsibility. On those trusty end-of-the-weekend evaluation sheets with questions to invite the happy or sad responses, came several scrawling critiques with words to praise the soul of humanity's heavenly destiny. Those same critiques denounced the value of earthly things, living things, life-giving things, created things. This was a legacy of Christianity's merger with first-century Gnosticism and twentieth-century fundamentalism. And the resulting biblical interpretation seemed to reveal clear choices by decisive people who sought an end to the journey with the pebble.

Yes, those weekend souls placing their wishes on angel wings were only a few, but my own pondering heart knew that they represented millions of Christians worldwide. I knew as I slid my skis up the white wonderland, that Christianity as a whole had long ago lost the pebble, or had purchased new shoes, or had been laid too low by the constant rub of this life. No wonder the world has not turned to Christians for answers when there is sickness and the threatened death of the planet.

And so the gray of my insides met the crest of our trail, the rise that signaled our turnaround. Soon we would slide to match the mountain's falling winter slopes. The very start of the descent dropped steeply, with uneven ruts and gashes in the snow cover. I chose to forget my gray mind, and I thought instead to push off hard into flight, to soar down that little canyon of snowflakes piled into pillows. I let go and I did soar grandly—for about thirty feet. I was magnificent for all of three seconds, when suddenly my right ski chose its own flight to the right and dropped into its own deep rut, angling away from the rest of my body, which would not slide equally to the right. I hung in the air for a bite out of time, like an Olympic ski jumper wedging the same air with skis turned outward. But without the slightest chance to swallow or even taste that air, I crumpled to the ground within a whiteout of winter's harsh embrace.

I lay there, having been brought back to earth so suddenly and feeling the sting of sharp-edged snowflakes in my ear and across my cheek. As I painfully balanced again over my skis and rose to my normal height, I studied the ski tracks leading down the mountainside, those same tracks I would have to take. The truth of those tracks spoke to me in my unfrozen ear, saying that skis were not wings, my earthly crossing would leave a trail, snow must part like lake water, and I would soon feel the pebble again while interpreting the Bible.

Truthful Words Are Good News

The Bible has been blamed for a lot of things, including leading us into the environmental crisis. Some environmentalists call us to move beyond the Bible in order to find the answers to our problems. Add to this the folks who believe the Bible calls us to forsake this world, and we have just about every imaginable way around a serious reading of the text itself. Consider the possibility that the disagreement may have less to do with the book than it has to do with taking sides and finger-pointing.

I am not very interested in the arguments over who or what is to blame. I would much rather get on with my life, living within an exciting world, retelling what to me will always be a thrilling story. Certainly the faith story for Christians is involved here, what with all the time spent in church or with television sermons, or all the mission work around the globe. But has the whole story been told? Has the whole story been read and understood? Have we listened with anticipation? Could we hear it again within a commitment to be honest with ourselves, to see the truth about our lives, to go eyeball to eyeball with the implications of our wastefulness and our addiction to possessions?

What I like most about my faith story, beginning with Genesis and continuing through my life today, is that when discovered through painful honesty, the story tells me that I am but a child. I am nursing and growing constantly, but I remain a child. I skip stones across the smooth surface of the planet like Tinker Toy buildings of the cities I have known. I run in green grass back in my hometown, chasing my friends with a cap gun in my hand. I lie down at night on my twin bed with my big brother in the bed next to me. I squeal with delight when Dad hands me a furry, brown puppy that pees on everything but the newspaper. When I read the Bible I do not have to be grown-up if being grown-up means that I am my own boss, my own man, having my own piece of the world.

This childlike nature must not be equated with immaturity or condescension ("trust me, you will understand better when you grow up"). I speak of an eager, adventuresome spirit with no self-conscious motive of protection for personal interests. This ideal spirit of the child cannot contain its impatience to learn and explore. This spirit retains an openness to God's Spirit, and always seems willing to unlearn in the presence of new truthfulness. And this same childlike nature somehow finds its freedom to choose creativity and new life, even in the face of past troubles, past abuses, past trauma, past disappointment, past failures, past violence.

And so it clearly falls within the eyesight and hearing and touch of this child dwelling inside us, to read again a text of the Bible that thoroughly leads us by the hand into a new land, a new character, a new reality, a new life. But only if we want to go, to change, to discover, to live differently, will the text take us into a new world. Thus the dilemma: our old world and the text must meet head-on. This is exactly why so many people, Christian and non-Christian alike, read the Bible and find nothing to change them. The Bible remains silent to all who would come to it without an old world to offer in exchange for something new. The Bible only speaks to us when we come to it with our heart in our hand, without our own answers, with dire need to face real-life problems, and with self on the platter. When we actually bring that much of ourselves to the text, the interface of the text and real life explodes into spiritual discovery, emotional upheaval, and even childlike joy.

So why do we not all rush into the text in order to find this new thing, this excitement? Because for most people the price proves to be too high. Most people are unwilling to part with self, to change fundamentally at their very core. Few of us are that desperate or that committed. No wonder much of society either scoffs at the Bible out of ignorance, or respects the Bible from a safe distance, or uses the Bible to preach what is already believed.

Let us together approach a text that may change us both, Mark l0:35-45. If you are uncertain about your commitment to hear this passage, simply skip to the next chapter of this book. If you simply want to listen in on someone else's conversation with the Bible, I will warn you right now that you will not hear the Bible's half of the conversation. I am not even sure that you will hear my half of the conversation. The child in me says, "Ready or not, here we go!"

This passage embarrasses me. I cannot read about how James and John ask Jesus such a stupid question without feeling embarrassed for them, as if it was me asking the question. "Jesus," I say, "I want you to do for me whatever I ask." (This already sounds like the way we Christians often pray. We forget that prayer is much more about what happens to us than what happens to God.) And Jesus says, "What is it you want?" So I say, "Let me sit at your right when you come into your glory."

If I am honest with myself and honest in the dialogue

with this passage, I must admit that my embarrassment comes from secretly identifying with James and John. I too want to have the glory. I too look to Jesus for personal gain. I am a groupie of sorts; I have my personal motives for claiming a Christian faith. God have mercy on me for automatically wanting to fill my own pockets, or to ride Jesus' coattails to heaven.

Where does this leave us Christians who tend to want all the things God could possibly give to us? Maybe like James and John we are acting like spoiled children, ever wanting more even though we have been given so much. Are we tired of all that God has already given us? Have we forgotten what God has already given us? Do we expect a constant flow of bounty when we spoil what we have already been given? James and John already had Jesus right in front of them, walking by their side, and speaking to them in kind and loving words. But they were not satisfied with the present. It was not real enough for them, they wanted some grand future. What we think we would sacrifice anything for—Christ's immediate presence—they found insufficient.

So what could possibly have been so important to them? If we pay careful attention to the story, we get some indication. James and John had gone to Jesus with their request without the knowledge of the other disciples. When the other disciples heard about the conversation, they became quite upset with James and John. Without knowing more of the background we must not draw hard and fast conclusions, but it seems likely that this incident grew out of the interpersonal dynamics among the disciples. It would be a safe bet to say that a sort of pecking order had been developing among the twelve. James and John were looking to get their bid for glory in early, and the strongly negative response of the others suggests that they too had invested in the subtle power plays of human social dynamics.

Again at this point in the story, let's be honest. The

behavior of the disciples is far from unusual. In fact, it is utterly typical. So if we express any shock or dismay, we most likely have our own power politicking to thank. And before we move to how Jesus handled this situation, let's recognize our own complicity. Let's admit our own get-ahead mentality. Let's register our own "I deserve it" thinking. And let's truly open ourselves to the vulnerability of being honest. By honesty I mean a total examination of our life's goals, our secret passions, and all the subtleties of our relationships. Doing this, we may want to rethink our desire to have Jesus present, for we may not want him to get that personal. All of a sudden we may be thankful to not have been one of those early disciples who were directly and personally confronted by Jesus' words.

If we still want to be honest and continue with the story, then we must openly confess that we are society. The Western world was built upon the ideals of the individual right to get ahead. Period. We must now truthfully say that we cannot divest ourselves of this legacy given to us at birth. We must say that there are countless ways, in every part of our lives, that we sacrifice other life forms and other human beings for our self-interest—often only for our convenience. And that prosperity has only compounded the severity with which we have abused the disadvantaged and raped the earth.

We must stop using Christianity as a false flag of truce. Christian people have been some of the worst abusers and rapists. Christian people have been some of the most dishonest people, living one way, while at the same time piously reading the text before us. Let us say with grieving hearts that we have brought our world—carried with bloodstained hands—into the presence of this text. Let us offer our world as a peace offering; may we lay it down and let it go, and then back away and stand naked before the text. If we still want God's glory and God's power, then we must know that we cannot own it as a possession. God's authority is much more, it is a transformation. Christ's words carefully given to the disciples are the words of transformation. We will not hear his words unless we are standing naked and empty-handed and longing for a new world, a new life, a new mind. Am I ready to hear Christ's words? Are you ready to hear Christ's words? Always a great risk, we must finally offer ourselves as the sacrifice instead of asking it of others.

Our brief story from Mark 10 draws to a climax when Jesus gathers all the disciples together in order to lay this whole matter of greatness to rest. No, Jesus' words are not necessarily profound in and of themselves, but if we hear them with open arms, honest hearts, and empty of our old selves, then his words fill our arms, burst our hearts, and replace emptiness with mission. In the presence of a life waiting to change, Jesus' words shatter the world left there at his feet and mandate other-worldly power. Jesus says, "It is not so among you." Such a simple and direct statement! Such a clear and definite pronouncement! Such a phrase of consequence for living! But what is not so among us? Rulers who lord it over others, great ones who are tyrants are no more. Self-serving dies with those words. Personal gain becomes meaningless with those words. Western society's birthright of individual freedoms gasps its last breath.

Yet this must not be read as some negative edict meant to shame us into obedient groveling. Jesus does talk about being first and about being great. Such power comes from no less than the mouth of God. And this power, this Godlike radiance, hails as divinity's pinnacle of earthly achievement. It also hails as the immediate antidote for human reconciliation. It also lies by the side of every person within arm's reach of a simple gesture of human kindness, the gift of wholeness offered—even pronounced—by God for every soul tattered and torn or drifting. This is good news! God's qualities are sprinkled like raindrops for anyone to run under!

So what is it to be first and to be great? Jesus says, "Be a servant. Be a slave. Give your life as I do." If this is the good news, then we may not want to stick around for the bad news. This is our world crashing headlong into the power of God; we find ourselves bound up all over again thinking like society. This voluntary servanthood or slavery *is* the good news and that *is* the truth! Anything less than voluntary servanthood or slavery is the bad news. If we intend to be Christians, to call ourselves after the One who has called us, then we must get this truth into our heads and our hearts. Jesus was not giving us a ball and chain, but a license for healing. Jesus was telling all followers everywhere that glorious power resides right in their fingertips and in their hands and in their arms and in their flesh-and-blood hearts. This good news becomes the foundation of all Christian creeds because this propels Jesus to the cross and his greatest act of service.

Why do we find it so difficult to see suffering and life-giving service as glorious attributes, as the privilege of every human soul? Because we learn early and we are taught throughout life in North America that service is only for folk heroes who give of their lives for others. We can only look up to someone as long as we put their lives above us, and this act nicely confirms our less than heroic ability. Because service shows rank—lower rank. And especially in a society touting equal rights while living without justice, without community, without a truthful love for all races and both sexes, we inherit an ingrained dishonesty. We are born into it and we do not even know that it has us. We do not even know what honest living looks or feels like.

Why do we not cherish for ourselves the life-giving service of Christ? Because we have accepted society's version of Christ which applauds service within acceptable parameters and within expected roles. In our society, service gains honor as allegiance to country, or it must filter through the inalienable rights of every individual. Christ has been watered down to the acceptable level of toxicity long before we Christians ever get to Mark 10. His words here then only penetrate our thinking partway. They are absorbed by our commitment to make him fit into a three-piece suit because that is what respectability looks like. And we are more concerned about respectability than about life-giving service.

If you are still with me in this conversation with the text, let us rejoice and sing hymns of praise together, for Jesus has shown us the way out of self-glorification. Jesus has shown us our falsehood. We may feel stripped of all that we know or knew to be real, but we no longer must search for dreams of grandeur and glory. The good news rests within our reach, and in this sense our dreams have come true, really true. But we must understand that we cannot dream two dreams simultaneously—if they are irreconcilable dreams. This text will not allow us to be great like Jesus only to a degree. One cannot dive into water without getting totally soaked. Jesus did not die halfway and neither can we. Jesus did not live by making deals with the Romans or the institutional faith. Neither can we. For every Christian who chooses to serve as Jesus did, there are hundreds, maybe thousands, who say they would like to. And there are hundreds, maybe thousands more, who will never get close enough to this text to even know that they must make a choice.

Finally, we must face the truth of our own lives, and we must hear the words of Jesus breathed into our own ears. It does not matter that the words were actually spoken almost 2,000 years ago. Truthful words never die, they only lie in wait for honest people to remember them. And their power stays dormant only if we turn away. We do stand in Jesus' presence when we stand before this text. Rather than believing in my God-given rights as a person living within a privileged society, I believe in transformation. I believe Jesus' words. They are now my words, my life, my death, my glory to be shared with all the world. Have you stuck with me and the text? What do you believe?

Of Black Bears, Pebbles, and Motorboats

"God so loved the world" and Christ entered, bursting history and shattering time. Can we have a God who does things halfway, even as we may want to accept only half the incarnation or half the creation or half the salvation? Can we divide up a God who wants to reconcile all things on this planet? Can we convince an oversized God that life-giving service should reign in and tether the horses next to the human watering hole?

Is it really so bad that we people of the earth always break things apart into manageable bites? We turn everything into packages that we can lift and carry and store within the warehouses of our minds. We know that some things do not fit in the boxes or would not taste right if savored long. But that, we say, is how the world is. It is an imperfect world, imperfect because it does not fit into our boxes or bites. We always claim to be caught between our boxes and the world's odd shapes and sizes. This is an inescapable dilemma that we have come to accept. Therefore, the only option remaining for us is to use our best judgment between our boxes and the world.

If we could peer into the boxes that other people carry, we would find the secrets that sculpt the nations, that probe the planets, that define meaningful life. We would see for ourselves the stargazers, the crystal balls, and the tea leaves of mortality. We would be filled by others' views of business and pleasure, of life's essentials. We, ourselves, may even become boxes carried by the people.

What? You say that you do not want to be defined within

someone's box? I am sorry for the assumption. You see, sometimes I cannot see humans anymore because the boxes block my view. So forgive me please, and I will show you that I am trying to carry an empty box, one that I can open without spoiling something I love. But that in itself becomes an impossible task, one which I happily plan to carry to my grave. I will do my best not to kill black bears, although I will need your help to stalk the one who does it for me. And I will not make big waves unless my box becomes heavy again and needs more than muscles to carry it through life. I promise you and myself that if my box needs angels' wings to carry it for its fullness, I will drop to the earth and embrace the soil until all the snows of the mountain melt and I have to walk home.

Jesus Christ created all things—the pebbles, the bears, even the components of motorboats. We do not have to believe it, though John and Paul and some other New Testament writers say so. God only creates good things, and this too we are not required to believe. But the book of Genesis started the rumor and I like it just fine. Creation is a funny thing. The Bible often says that people take it in reverse, like my car when I am not careful. Boats flying by me on the way to Prairie Portage say that they are going forward, but I know when cars are backing up because it has happened to me. Those vehicles in reverse are fueled by non-biodegradable fossil fuels collecting in the campsite mounds of the wilderness.

Creation must be a big word because it takes up so much space in the Bible, but *salvation* probably runs a photo finish. You see, *creation* was not a big enough word by itself because people found their boxes. Jesus had to begin the creation process all over again, a re-creation which began with a small band of human followers who needed to learn the truth about greatness. Some of Jesus' followers have learned, but many still have not learned. Even the life-giving lesson of the cross was not enough to show some that Jesus meant every word he said in Mark 10. Whether we call Jesus the Creator or the Re-creator, it is all an act of service—life-giving service and life-making service that extends in every direction, far past the human watering hole.

Colossians says it perhaps the best. The cross, that holy symbol of salvation and re-creation, lights the stage of all life's history with the act of Jesus reconciling all things to God. Here is where the blood of God seals the final fate of the world. Yes, God does love the world.

Perhaps I should fill my right hip pocket wherever I go in life. Or should I fill my soul with pebbles? Does it take that many well-placed pebbles to grind out the truth of life as service? A re-creation process as thorough as Christ's would surely exchange at least one pebble for every box we carry, and it would forever remind us that God can never be chopped up into bite-sized pieces. The God of creation and salvation cannot be sized down to fit into human boxes which are held and not released in the presence of the One who tells us how to be great.

Now the last word on service might take the form of a question. That is, how far are we to follow Jesus? At what point along the road shall we stop and eat a snack, build a fort, sleep easy, and treat the world about us as the "Gentiles" do? Or, if you do not like that question, here is another. When shall we stop laying down our lives? When we are out of high school? When we can afford fast machines—when the last wilderness is overrun? Or here is a third and final choice. When and where can we take the pebble from our shoe?

Jesus could surely tell us. So where is he when we really need him?

Find the black bear, for her death may claim the permanence of the pebble. And Jesus may always be found at the cross.

Christis the image of the invisible God,
  The firstborn of all creation.
    For in him all things in heaven and on earth were created!

Christ is before all things.
In Christ all things hold together.
In Christ the fullness of God was pleased to dwell.

Through Christ all things were reconciled to God,
  Whether on earth,
    Or in heaven,
By making peace through the blood of his cross.

                    Colossians 1:15-20
                    author's paraphrase

Chapter 9

Nurtured in Nonviolence

A Loss of Humanity

Violence takes many forms. Some people may not want to avoid violence, for the absence of violence creates a demand on them. Violence reflects a need in us—as if emotions could tell the mind how to find the way to fulfillment. Violence does not describe how we normally see ourselves, but rather how we see the other person, or how we see the world in general.

We do not easily own up to violence, but it easily owns us. We like to see violence as something dark and outside in the night, away from the house where we live. At home with all the lights on, we do not recognize the colorless, odorless violence, that like carbon monoxide filters into our bodies from engines running on the fuels of human desire. We tend to define violence rather narrowly when it comes to ourselves, saying that it is a willful act, specific and intentional, our personal choice. With this understanding of violence we are able to objectify it, classify it, and notarize it.

This violence that we can see and point to and read about in the morning news, this violence that does not invade our breakfast table as a sit-down guest—this is the violence that holds little real threat to the integrity of life on our planet. The far greater threat—the potential destruction of life itself—comes from the violence within us. For inside us resides the denial, the million reasons why we do not feel responsible for the illness of the planet, why we do not feel responsible for the destructive forces of our politics or our pleasures. This amazing ability to blame violence, destruction, pollution, rape, murder, and extinction on the system rises like an ocean tide, allowing us to absolve ourselves of all but a vague uneasiness about our personal lifestyles and our personal violence.This violence within us—the reality of our self-interest, that all-encompassing needfulness— births and feeds the process that finally kills all things. Because we are unsatisfied by what we have and by what we are, the world has become a dangerous place in which to live. Because we have aggressively sought to fulfill our desires and have imposed our wills upon each other and the earth with almost every action, we no longer even recognize the violence. You see, violence lives within the management of our relationships. We place our measure of meaning on every aspect of the web of life, we choose after our personal interests, and we are therefore violent.

I am intentionally weaving a broad definition of violence, a definition that implicates us all. This definition says that violence has everything to do with human hierarchy and everything to do with seeking our greatness by society's norm (James and John style, Mark 10:35-37). So, if we speak of violence as something that happens or as something that we do, we should recognize this as the outgrowth of attitudes of violence, belief systems that are inherently violent, and a self-understanding that fosters violence. Violence occurs anytime a person, an animal, or an object of matter is changed, controlled, or manipulated for our personal or corporate gain without full regard for its integrity as a divinely valued piece of creation. Any such manipulation rises from the bitter soil of our inner battles with self.

For us to think that a part of creation does not have great worth aside from our use of it as humans, or that it might go to waste if we do not use it, have it, or hold it—this feeds the attitude of violence. We might even say that we have killed something in our minds. Therein is the homicide of our true humanity, for no longer can we say that we are living in God's garden as servants and protectors.

Portage Bivouac

It happened on a late June afternoon. Our little band of voyagers was making headway through the final passage of lakes bordering the edge of the Quetico Provincial Park in Ontario. The day had begun on Kashipiwi, a lake as long and thin as hot taffy melting as it is being pulled. What a stretch of lakes and trails we had meandered across to find ourselves prepared to cross North Bay of Basswood Lake. Our sights were aimed from west to east, and we rested in the wake of a rocky butte that sheltered us from a sudden easterly wind. We abruptly turned aside our thoughts of a leisurely glide through the bay and began to anticipate a heavy workout of wind and waves.

Our eyes were uneasily fixed upon the eastern skyline as dirty gray clouds fought among themselves for the right to be first in line to roll at us. Until that moment of stormy contemplation, the day had been so calm and uneventful that we felt unseasoned for the coming challenge. To breathe hard into the wind and test the fibers of our wild pleasure on the tops of whitecaps would have been one response to the encroaching storm. To huddle in safety and laugh at the clouds from a boulder house along the shore would have been another. But it was the indecision that was killing us; the lure of the flight into potential danger held relentless against our cautious daydreams of safety.

The deadlock was broken by our focus on an island well out into North Bay. Four hundred, maybe five hundred yards out into the bay that big island looked friendly and beckoned us. We knew we had to risk at least that much of the bay. We knew we could find shelter from the storm behind the island's rocky tree line, in her inner sanctuary from all the easterly brew the skies could muster. But mostly, the island was an excuse to get us beyond our initial fear, to get us out there on the waves where we could test our skill. It was a half commitment—like marriage for those who might end a relationship rather than live together through their pain.

Once out on the bay, we were caught up in the excitement of the water, as I knew we would be. So we passed by the island and drove hard for the far shore, always glancing side to side to carefully gauge the progress of the other canoes in our group, while earnestly longing for the eastern shore to enlarge itself and draw us close. The pile of the waves constantly under our keels, the fierce wind washing our faces, the sidelong glances, and the pressing stare into the angry clouds that twisted and billowed even more severely than the waves: all this bore down upon our ability to maintain an equilibrium and balance our load atop the depths of North Bay. This time our wild abandon paid off, for we made it into our haven—a tiny inlet to the east of the bay—just as the storm hit.

The shore of the inlet was also the beginning of the portage trail leading to the next lake, so we loaded up our packs and canoes and headed up the trail. I was the last in line, and I hauled the canoe up onto my shoulders just as the hail began. As long as we were in the forest, we were protected somewhat from the wind. But the hail seemed to find us even among the trees. That was the first time I carried a canoe as my protection against hailstones. The marble-size hail came down hard and fast. I made sure my fingers were inside the canoe gunwales to protect them from being pounded by the small white pellets.

I did not realize that while I was enjoying the protection of my canoe, on the far side of the portage trail where the storm was truly raging, one member of our party was caught without the protection of either a canoe or the woods. Telling about it later, she said she freaked. She was standing there all alone, wearing a T-shirt and shorts. The hail seemed merciless; she momentarily lost her senses. Fortunately it was not long before another member of our group found her, and together they quickly retreated back up the portage trail and into the relative safety of the woods.

So our little band of storm travelers happened to gather mid-portage to exchange excitedly our differing views about the severity of the storm. With the hail still pounding us and with lightning flashing all around us, we judiciously sought out the only semi-level spot of woods we could find. As the rain became a downpour, we tied up a rain tarp in record time. Even as the wind blew and the tarp whipped around, we unpacked the stove. Someone braved the storm and ran for lake water, and in ten minutes we were drinking the most satisfying chicken noodle soup I have ever tasted.

What a crazy afternoon. We huddled there in midsummer with all our warm clothes on, topped with raincoats and rain pants, and watched the storm settle in. Though it was an uncomfortable place to bivouac, no one complained. As the afternoon turned into evening we looked with dismay at the possible tent sites. There were none. There was not a level piece of ground within any reasonable hiking distance. The woods were thick, and of course, it was very wet. What a crazy afternoon indeed, as we repeatedly nudged the tarp's swelling belly of water so that it gushed to the ground just away from our packs and our sitting area. Thoughts of what could have been were uneasily sifting through all our minds. Crazy could have become dangerous and downright deadly had that storm met us out on the bay. I had to wonder why I take risks like that, what moves me to push the limits of human existence, and what could possibly justify our defiant brush with eternity?

It was a crazy afternoon, and one worth contemplating between lightning bolts. Violence dwells in the sky as a thunderhead builds to gigantic proportions. But this is a different violence than humans know. The storm has no malevolent spirit; searing a living thing to instant death by lightning is not a conscious act. The storm bore no wrath or grudge against the paddlers crossing North Bay. Certainly there are powerful forces in nature that at times bring great destruction; one need only witness the aftermath of a tornado or an earthquake to know this. Volcanoes erupt, rivers flood, hurricanes crash against the coastlands, avalanches suddenly descend the mountainside. A thunderstorm may seem almost benign when compared with other natural forces. The elements of nature are unsettled; ours is not the task to control nature or to rage against these natural forces. Yet we do have a task—a challenge—and that is to listen, to understand, to learn from and to work with the natural processes, even in their violent forms.

It is the attitude we bring to all our encounters with nature that harbors within us a hope or a desperate needfulness. Count the last one hundred times your life touched a part of the natural world, affected the bloom of flowers or the lives of trees, or simply sang with the sparrows at dawn. If we allow for honesty, then we each will know that the greatest disaster is not the natural one, but an unnatural one. And that is the disaster inside the human heart.

As evening descended on our group huddled there under that rain tarp, the storm finally passed. In the last remaining hour of daylight we packed up and drove the canoes hard across the water to a campsite. Looking up at that sky as we paddled the last stretch before dark, we could still see the twisting, churning clouds. But also there, spanning the whole sky, was a brilliant rainbow in full color. We stopped our work momentarily to gaze in wonder and to contemplate its meaning. We were tired, wet, and hungry, having narrowly escaped the worst of the storm. We were still anxious about where we would find our night's rest. But that view of the rainbow became our hope and our promise—a promise of God to all creation.

Ingall's Creek

Ingall's Creek is about thirty feet wide as it tumbles down the eastern slope of the Cascade Mountains. I am sitting atop a Douglas fir log that has nicely laid itself across the creek as a bridge. The log is two feet in diameter and I dangle my legs over its sides, leaving about two more feet of clearance between my boots and the rushing water. It is springtime, and the creek is full of snow melt. Last night the water level dropped almost four inches with the refreezing of the snowpack in the cold mountain darkness. I am only up about 4,000 feet, but I see that I am still surrounded by snow on both sides of the creek and in every direction. It is a glorious, sunny day, and I sense in my spirit that Ingall's Creek is once more on the rise.The water beneath me plays a constant tune, an orchestra of waltzing fluid. The rocks here will not dance and so the water must cascade into them, crash all around them, and liven the world with music. By evening the one rock on which I perch to catch some of the water for drinking, will again swell over with the rush of snow melt from high on the sides of these mountains. The water's tune muffles the sound of the forest and creates an almost surreal cacophony of the sounds normally heard here. Birds are singing, but I only hear the sharp notes and the ones trilled close to my ears. Once or twice a red squirrel chatters, but only an alert listener can make out the sound. All else that remains here seems dormant, though it is spring and all is greening and budding to life.

This is a solitary place, especially now, before the rush of summer campers. The trail here still lies partially covered with snow, and I sit here staring up at a white and glistening peak. Even on its steep sides the patches of snow are still large and its few trees look small and green in contrast with the white snow. Its height and the height of the other peaks around me dwarf this place where I ride the log over Ingall's Creek. No one else rides the log here. I squint in the bright sunlight as ants, both huge and tiny, cross and recross the span, as if wishing the human obstacle in their path would be removed. But I will stay awhile as my bottom half grows numb against this ancient fir bridge. For what other human will herald the beauty here if I will not?

Over at the campsite my tent nestles low upon the forest floor. Giant trees all around me loom hundreds of feet in the air, straight as arrows shooting toward the sun. My tent pegs prick the earth among silent root systems buried in loamy soil pocked with rocks of all sizes. My temporary home is hemmed in by these trees. I can roughly see the path that leads to somewhere else. But in this solitary place I find that it is easy to forget about the path, even to forget about my journey here yesterday. I have to remind myself of these things; otherwise I could never leave this place. Yesterday as I settled here, I was somewhat disappointed, for I had hoped for a more open place. Perhaps I am too long a prairie dweller. But then I found my sitting log across the very bosom of the creek, and now I have grown to love these trees that almost hug me with their own special solitary strength.

I slept last night upon the lengthy anchoring limbs of these hulking giants. It was a silent sleep, for everything beyond the water music held still upon the command of the trees. Even the wind here must obey the trees' command, so it slows to a breeze filtering the cold night air. I awoke at times throughout the night and thought I would catch the trees inattentive of their duties. But every time I opened my eyes, I only experienced a calm darkness. Every time I listened into that deep black night, I heard only water music. The trees wished it so, and today they are my closest friends.

Finally the log across the creek proved more wooden than my body, so I now dangle my feet close to the glowing embers of this morning's fire. I must admit that I forgot the fire and slighted it a bit, for it crackles and claims a small music of its own. (Though I also should say that after a winter's blanket of snow, the wood prefers to smoke and not to flame.) I have become accustomed to campfire smoke over the years, for it seems that thousands of campfires have come and gone through my memories. Each one has been like a kiss of sunlight to light a dreary night, or to steal away the winter cold.

This experience on Ingall's Creek draws me into nonviolence, and nurtures it into my being. I learn a way of being in this world because I am here. It is hard to explain, though it makes perfect sense to the growing things around me as I write this message. The letters forming words on this page fall from two hundred foot heights like tiny fir cones, they splash like the water drops splayed out from the creek's raucous rush, and they crackle like baby embers spit from the fire. These, creation's own language, say that there is no cause for fear, there is no cause for impatience, there is no cause for greed, there is no cause for power over something or someone. I rest in that thought, because it is the hope that guides my soul.

In the days before my trip up Ingall's Creek, my life had become frenzied to the point of violence. My mind and spirit had taken mortal wounds from all the demands placed upon me. I know the rage that comes with frustration, and I know the deep depression that comes from weariness and resentment. And all the time these trees along Ingall's Creek have simply guarded this place and held it close until my arrival. Speak to the trees of your anger. Scream the obscenities that lurch in your bowels. Flail at the water with pounding fists of rage, and it will not know your pain, it will not strike you in return, it only sings its journey downward to the sea. The birds will only fly from you as you weep loudly. But the ground will hold you, the breeze will soothe you, the stillness will calm you, and the seeds of violence planted deeply by human intention will die, for they are not tended in this garden. You see, the ingredients of the human experience that mix to form cultural structures and belief systems are so easily poisoned by greed and power. We are left with almost no choice but to become innately violent. These are known only to the human species. If we would, we could unlearn a lot of what goes wrong for us by letting all of creation teach us in its way.

Reconciliation

Christians are a violent people. Across this world Christians are known for their violence. Christians have co-opted entire cultures in the name of Jesus. That is a supremely violent act. Christians have fought countless wars under the banner of Christ's cross. Christians have oppressed the poor in every nation where they have become wealthy and powerful. Christians have often seized every opportunity to be racist and sexist. Within the church we find bigots of every kind. Christians everywhere have destroyed the natural world God created.

As if all these forms of violence are not enough, we have

the audacity to continue evangelizing the human population of this world. Evangelize to what? What message could we ever hope to bring to other peoples that they could possibly hear above our violence? One might think evangelism would be a deeply positive experience, like telling a very wonderful and hopeful story, but violence is not good news. And, it is nothing new. The people of our world already know violence. What could we Christians possibly think we have to offer to others by adding our violence to theirs?

Evangelism as used in the New Testament simply means "good news." It is the good news of Christ as we read in his own words in Luke 4:43, "I must proclaim the good news of the [reign] of God to the other cities also; for I was sent for this purpose." The Greek word we translate into English by the words *good news* has the same root as the word *evangelism.*

We have already said that violence is not good news, certainly not the news that God came into the world to proclaim! So why do Christians continue to believe that they can live violently and yet speak about good news? Well, there you have it, something that I have never understood and probably never will. I know that I cannot whip my daughter into submission and then expect her to treat others nonviolently. The old adage does not say that words speak louder than actions, but just the opposite.

On a recent flight from Dallas to Toronto, I sat beside a man who directs a branch office of the Humane Society. He told me something that I have not been able to forget. He said they have discovered that often an abused animal is an indication of the existence of abuse within the family system of the animal's owner. I would never have concluded that on my own, but when he spoke of this violence cycle, it made all too much sense. The message seems very clear. We simply cannot do violence without having it repeated or played out in some way among people, animals, or in nature.

If we Christians want to do evangelism based on the good news of God's sovereign rule in this world, we had better begin with ourselves. We would be wise to face the kind of news that our lifestyles tell. Where this is not good news, may we have the wisdom and the grace to repent of our violence.

I have always been baffled by how the biblical message really brings such good news until it gets skewered and all the juice gets cooked right out of it over a slow Christian fire. Yes, another form of our violence shows itself in the way we abuse the biblical text. When I was growing up we were reminded never to take Christ out of Christmas, which is a very good thought. But someone forgot to remind Christians not to take Christ out of Christianity. When we live violently, we live as if Christ's life and teaching have no bearing on our lives, as if they have no power to make a real difference in our world and bring no good news and hope to an already violent world.

Would someone please tell me why we scare "the hell" out of people with our Christian witness and then later bomb "the hell" out of them, pummeling the earth in the name of Christ and eventually leaving little resources for those who have survived our evangelism and our bombing? It simply makes no sense to "save" someone's soul and also support the military machinery that kills them later. If we commit to what we believe and we preach what we believe, and this all remains founded upon the violence undergirding our lifestyles, then for what can we possibly have "saved" them?

But enough cynicism. The truth remains that Christ lived and taught nonviolence, and that headlines the good news of God's sovereign rule. Under God's rule here and now, as Christ brought it into being, relationships of all kinds are brought into harmony. To be "in Christ" as Paul speaks of it in the New Testament, means to live at one with Christ, to live and die nonviolently, to live and speak of reconciliation. Though this book is not a Bible study, we must look at one text noted briefly in Chapter 8. This text clearly sums up the good news and truly nurtures us humans into the way of nonviolence.

In writing to the church at Colossae, Paul describes Christ in the following way,

> He is the image of the invisible God, the firstborn of all creation; for in him all things in heaven and on earth were created, things visible and invisible, whether thrones or dominions or rulers or powers— all things have been created through him and for him. He himself is before all things, and in him all things hold together. He is the head of the body, the church; he is the beginning, the firstborn from the dead, so that he might come to have first place in everything. For in him all the fullness of God was pleased to dwell, and through him God was pleased to reconcile [to God] all things, whether on earth or in heaven, by making peace through the blood of his cross. (Colossians 1:15-20)

Such a powerful text could fill many pages with commentary, but I only want to lift up the last verse. In this verse, Paul proclaims Christ's mission as the reconciliation of all things to God through Christ's death on the cross. If I believe this, how then can I call myself Christian and do violence to anything? How can I say with Paul that I am "in Christ" but live destructively, undoing Christ's very work? This is tough, because I really do live destructively. I am a part of a destructive society, and I must live with this reality. I shudder to think of all the ways I benefit from the oppression of people and the natural world. The food I eat, the car I drive, the computer with which I write—all these things and many more point to me as an over-consumer of the earth's resources. While I have, others have not. While I buy, the earth dwindles. This opposes the myth of capitalism, in which the market economy thrives because more buying power is believed to be better. And the myth of capitalism finds its legitimacy from the even larger myth that says there is enough for me to keep getting more, that the earth's resources are ours to manipulate and to exhaust.

The Bible has a myth too, one that says God owns the earth, that God made the universe, and that God reconciles all things. We must choose which myth we will believe, for these two myths simply are not compatible. One disproves the other. And only one will identify us as Christians who live their faith, a faith based on God's story and God's life as written and proclaimed by Paul.

This one verse in Colossians would betray all the prior uses of Christ's cross as cover for violence in any form. This one verse would signify to all Christians that the good news culminates in an act of nonviolence. The cross, that undisputed Christian symbol, contains in itself the indictment of every violent act. If Christ's work is to reconcile all things, then we surely must count as violence the destruction of the earth.

Where lives the hope for an alternative to a violent heart? Hope lives in the one true myth that claims reconciliation for all things. And because humanity, above all else, needs reconciliation, we humans must claim the text before us. Christ is our hope, for in Christ reconciliation enters our world as the victor over violence. I too can be changed, reconciled. I too can make different choices about how I live. I too can become one "in Christ," a reconciling agent in the world and on behalf of the world.

It would seem clear, following this line of reasoning, that it is the Christian church that is most in need of evangelization. For the Christian church sorely needs to hear again the good news of Christ's reconciliation of all things.

Yet it would also seem that the Christian church has not

found Ingall's Creek. There has been no solitary hike up the deep ravine cut away by centuries of patient water. There has been no discovery of winter's old snow melting into the relentless green of mountain spring. In other words, the Christian church has not discovered the nurture of the earth to counter the violence of that human institution. People who would seek the way of Christ, an arid wanderer, without the resolve of his loving ways, are a people without a log bridge from which to dangle feet over the water's gift of life. How can we then stop the flow of another kind of rushing like water down a mountainside, but not like Ingall's Creek? Violence also can become a roaring to replace all other music in our souls.

How can we have the patience to rise almost as unnoticed throughout the sunlight hours as the water inching over the drinking rock at the Ingall's Creek campsite? How can we know another swelling inside our hearts that leaves no space for the seeding of violent attitudes? Might it just be possible for the Christian church to know that the divine-human exchange does not flow in the direction of self-centered salvation but in the direction of a singing creek, tumbling wildly downward as an act of self-giving? In this self-giving, we would most likely find a union of divine and human intent, certainly a reconciliation of salvation proportions.

View from Thunder Point

For many miles Knife Lake divides the territories of Ontario and Minnesota. Its crystal waters bridge the gap separating two countries. The surface waters tend the shorelines both north and south, tend the islands cupped in the lake's buoyant surroundings, and prove the testing ground for the many shapes of canoe hulls parting the brow of its waves. Knife Lake is a day's journey by canoe from the nearest road. Portages, some long and some short, also create a distance from motors, telephones, and pavement. Knife Lake may have earned its name from the long bladelike shape of its body nestled in a cutting fashion within its small crevasse rifted in the Canadian Shield.

On a clear sunlit day, with only slight breezes to ruffle the feathery leaves of the aspen along the shore, the paddler is welcomed by the lake into a vast, wet ecology. Mallard ducks or Mergansers will often play at the far western edge of the lake where waters whisk away down a rock slide rapid.

Entering the lake's environment from the west you shove off from the lip of the rapids and glide into the calm of a narrow bay. Within about a mile you can paddle alongside the islands that were home to Dorothy Molter, who was nicknamed with love and respect, "the Root Beer Lady." The last living resident of the Boundary Waters, Dorothy died in December 1986 at age seventy-nine. Now her islands show little sign of ever having been inhabited. But for those who visited Dorothy's Isle of Pines while she was still making and selling root beer, Knife Lake and those islands will always be her home.

Heading east another few miles, the lake begins to widen as it prepares itself for division. On a wide stretch of water resembling the mouth of a great river, Knife Lake parts and moves both north and south. The land mass, towering rocky and green 200 feet above the surface of the water, stands tall as a buttress, heralding the waters' divide. Thunder Point is the name of the imposing mass, crediting the rise with a well-deserved dignity.

Though I have hiked to the top of Thunder Point many times, I still cannot pass by without a few moments on its summit. I have found no other place in all the Boundary Waters where I can gain such a perspective on my past journey. The view is simply breathtaking. It provides me with a renewed sense of my personal merit compared to the expansive ecosystem before me. It gives to me a transformed understanding of value, the value of life's system of living things.

The power of Thunder Point leaks from cracks in its rocks and from the wash of soil. It rubs itself raw with open roots of ancient fir trees, and it cries from the mouths of red squirrels bounding in broad and sweeping boughs of white pine. The power trickles one drop at a time into the heart and mind of the paddler. The view to the west transforms the wide, but ever-narrowing waterway into a runway for behemoths from heaven. It is no longer just a pathway for paddlers of earthly fare, but is now a smooth surface, pock-marked with character by the islands and destined for graceful takeoffs by God's messengers heralding the splendor of creation.

Ages past saw the weight of centuries old ice carving roughly and deeply the depths of the lake, its bays, and arms. But that same cold tonnage carefully crafted and touched only softly the sides of Thunder Point, perhaps buoying it up with the joy of frozen crystals. So the vista chronicles a journey both recent and long past. The day's trek over wisps of waves shining in the sun reminds the paddler of the grace of the glacier that once both crossed and carved the same route.

The view from Thunder Point shapes the way we understand water travel, for there on that mountain of rock and soil one touches and feels the water from a greater perception of the living earth. A larger view of life becomes possible because we are given to seeing, perhaps for the first time, a mixture of time and timelessness, the interplay of water with air, with green, with rock, with blue sky, and with bright sun. The earth and her environment hold up for us a perspective of living time, the slow process of life. It ever tells us a story of living and dying and living again. This grand vision may, if we allow it, implant itself in our thinking, and there grow old together with our new understanding of patience, even the knowledge of divine patience in the person of the Creator.

Like the view from Thunder Point, we humans must climb higher in order to see a new vision. We must look out over the distance we have traveled and integrate a broader understanding of our living environment that will shape hope into our future with the earth. We must be able to see far beyond the day-to-day journey, which only understands short-term solutions and monthly balance sheets. We must be able to peer out over more distant horizons, stepping beyond our defensive reactions to the new call for eco-justice, leaving behind our antiquated views of human dominance.

We must reclaim Isaiah's vision of the lion lying down with the lamb—only let us know ourselves to be the lion and God's good creation to be the lamb. We are at the point in the story of the Christian church for Christians of all stripes to see this vision from atop Thunder Point, to view the prophetic vista as the hope of the future, the nurturing presence of God's reconciliation, the healing of the human spirit.

Even the historic peace churches must climb the mountain and taste new air, touch higher green, and bask in the close sunlight of altitudes that are to date unknown. For the peace churches have always remained narrow in vision, with sights set too low upon the ground. Let them now proclaim their pacifism for more than one species of life! Let them now cry to the eagle circling the heights, "Give us your sight, for ours remains locked up in lowly stations of Christ's cross held too close to see its dominance over all the landscape." Let the Christians of peace teach and learn. Let them teach the nonviolence they know to all other Christians, and let them learn a whole new approach to life taught by the earth and all the creatures of the earth. Let them therefore discover a new wholeness, a new energy, and new life to expand their nonviolent ways.

May we all drop our blinders when next we open our sacred text, a text that is sacred in the sense that it tells a holy story of God creating and reconciling. When we climb out of the air lock of our hermeneutical holding patterns, we will discover that the biblical vision has always been a lofty one. Walter Brueggeman wrote sixteen years ago in his book, *Living Toward a Vision:*

> The central vision of world history in the Bible is that all of creation is one, every creature in community with every other, living in harmony and security toward the joy and well-being of every other creature. In the community of faith in Israel, this vision is expressed in the affirmation that Abraham is the father of all Israel and every person is his child (Genesis 15:5; Isaiah 41:8, 51:2). Israel has a vision of all people drawn into community around the will of its God (Isaiah 2:2-4). In the New Testament, the church has a parallel vision of all persons being drawn under the lordship and fellowship of Jesus (Matthew 28:16-20; John 12:32) and therefore into a single community (Acts 2:1-11). As if those visions were not sweeping enough, the most staggering expression of the vision is that all persons are children of a single family, members of a single tribe, heirs of a single hope, and bearers of a single destiny, namely, the care and management of all of God's creation.

When this vision—this view from life's Thunder Point— becomes the vision guiding our lives, then evangelism will have meaning. When we step up to a higher plane, above violence and attitudes of violence, we will have something profound to say to all the world, something ultimately divine as in the words of Paul to the Colossians. God's reconciliation will be our vision and our work.

Last of all, let us simply breathe a prayer for mercy. Let us hold into our bosom the love that surrounds us. Let us climb up to new realms of personal awareness based on a love of all things. This is a time for confession, a time to end the game of superlatives that can only describe a false sense of our soul. As we sit at our tables in our comfortable homes, let us look to the breakfast partner reflecting the shadows of our desires. May the partner and the reflection bloom into flowers on the mountainside, adorning the view of Knife Lake's western horizon, and may they blossom brilliantly in the music flowing from Ingall's Creek.

May we see from our blooming place Isaiah's vision, and by God's grace, may we be looking at our own reflection.

On the Messiah shall God's Spirit rest.
Judging not by eyesight or by hearing.
The Messiah shall judge by righteousness,
> *The poor,*
> *The meek with equity,*
> *The wicked with death.*

Righteousness and faithfulness shall clothe this one,
> *And the wolf shall live with the lamb,*
> *The leopard shall lie down with the kid,*
> *The calf with the lion,*
> *The cow with the bear.*
>> *A little child shall lead them.*

They will not hurt or destroy on all my holy mountain;
> *For the earth will be full of the knowledge of God*
>> *As the waters cover the sea.*

> *Isaiah 11:3-9*
> *author's preface*

Chapter 10

God's
Justice
Ecology

The Storehouses of Winter

The last day of 1991 proved to be mild in the Canadian Rockies. Of course it was winter, with deep snow at all the higher elevations. We were prepared to enjoy every inch of it while gliding up and down the slopes on cross-country skis. The temperature hovered around 20 degrees Fahrenheit, which was a pleasant surprise since we had expected the kind of cold that cracks brittle things and creaks underfoot. Still, the day was crisp and clear, just as high elevation winter days are supposed to be. Leaving behind our heavier clothing, the four of us clipped into our skis and slid away from the trailhead.

The moment we entered the woods we knew a different climate, one hushed and unbroken by sounds of any kind. If we stood silent on our skis and held in our heavy breathing, winter herself was there to communicate her calming, floating voice of stillness. And in the stillness everything visible and everything cloaked underneath the snow seemed at rest, in a dormancy that bordered on comatose slumber. We were the unrestful. We entered at the risk of disturbing something we could not comprehend. Yet it was winter, the gracious host, who said, "Welcome."

The ski trail was narrow and meandered upward through the sweep of evergreen branches. We labored at times, overheated, just as we shivered occasionally as a bit of sweat dried in the light wind of a downhill run. The experience of outdoor winter activity always threatens the balance between hot and cold, challenging a delicate body's system of survival. And there lurks at least part of the attraction to a winter excursion into the higher altitudes: some wayward souls search for the chance to feel that they have come home to a white hearth and a deep, downy cushion of shelter. The oneness of our temporal, fragile existence and the lusty, bitter cold of winter's death scares all life forms into submission.

But some winter days are meant for celebrating the warmth of winter, for even in winter temperatures usually remain within the range of life support, as long as care is taken to retain the reserves of heat from metabolism and exercise. So this surely was a day to celebrate the season of dormancy. The season of rest, the season of white insulation, the season of hibernation, the season when some animals bear their young in dens of silence and safety—this was our chosen day to stalk the joys of the cold winter.

Yet often, winter symbolizes the chill in our hearts. We tend to let our images of bitterness define what we do not understand. We see in winter the struggle of survival, and we judge the process within our negative sense of discomfort or cruel reality. The human tendency to romanticize a simplistic concept of nirvana inevitably includes all the luxuries of warmth and love and peace. Nature's harsh reality becomes for us the symbol of evil, of a fallen world.

Unfortunately, we lose a deeper perspective on life when we define life by our desires. Winter, death, and tragedy—while not often our choice—are certainly the stuff life is made of. And we would be farther along the trail of wisdom if we could acknowledge that these are not inconsistencies, but that they are a part of God's world. Without them, we could not know summer, living, and joyful surprise.

Winter moves across the landscape like an annual death march and strikes the chords of spring's slumber. This resonant vibration bares an exemplary scene of justice—God's way of providing—a way not always understood from the human perspective.

With the midday sun shining brightly, we made a place for our lunch amid the snows of that mountain cold. Crystals gleamed in the orange light from the sun's reflection upon winter's tablecloth, as if placed there to grace our simple meal with decor unbounded. To think that the same sun in months ahead would transform all the bitter ice and snow now killing the unprepared, destroying the disabled and weakened! This transformation to yield the bounty of streams and rivers rushing down, this would be the outcome of struggle. And though I shiver in the gray light of winter and some time will lose my ability to live within its chill, I must acknowledge that I am fully a part of its cycle, that I am fully a part of death, that I am fully a part of tragedy. Knowing this, my sadness will always turn to the joys of being a living part of the whole. As long as I have breath, I will return from sorrow to praise a providential God for providing the needs of the world. Thankfully, God's world and God's justice will always reach beyond my own.

The Hand of God

During the early '70s I was fulfilling a two-year term of

service for the church in an inner city on the West Coast. Along with the other young adults in my unit, our grueling schedules kept us in almost constant contact with the children and youth of the city. Occasionally we escaped and found some precious time to ourselves, away from the pressure of young dependents. One such occasion found us far up the coast and across the border for two days of camping in British Columbia.

Following a pleasant evening around the campfire and a good night's sleep, our whole group was rejuvenated and prepared for a day of exploration. Three of us looked up into those coastal mountains and caught sight of a small stream leaping its way down the mountain in waterfalls and gushing rapids. Our fate for the day was sealed as we set our hearts on climbing up to where the water could only descend.

The day was not hot, which made the climbing easier. We drank the stream water when needed, and we steadily worked our way up, not heeding the times when the spray and splash of water seemed to signal discretion or danger. We were filled with the sense that we alone were a human presence in that place, and that we alone had ever touched the rocky staircase leading up the water pathway. On either side the forest huddled close to the stream, like bed partners on a centuries-old night's sleep. Rip Van Winkle's years multiplied until the years did not matter anymore, for they would seem to come and go forever.

In this way the forest gave us confidence; it felt like the net below a high wire act. We knew that at any time we could abort the challenge that had called to us earlier that morning from the safety of the campsite. At any time we could step from our watery rocks and slippery toeholds onto the carpet of forest floor with trees to hug and to hold, trees that were anchored well into the steep angle of the mountainside.

But the challenge—the lusty side of life—lay with the water and the rock. And instead of decreasing as we climbed higher, the urgency within our spirits intensified as we scanned the horizon from the height and as we peered deeply down the channel through which we had ascended. There were times when the only way up the rock ledge was through the very path of water. And at these times the water's cold encircling our hands would almost numb the power in our grip, numb the grasp for life, numb our hold on the dream of rising in full oneness with the mountain's streaming thirst.

Late morning brought us to a relatively level ledge of rock on which the stream pooled off to our left. The rock itself was a magnificent granite step for some giant spirit of the mountain. Or was it the throne for some goddess of the forest whose nighttime ramblings would bid her rest awhile by moonlight? It was a place pockmarked by the centuries of grinding water, rough and uneven upon closer gaze.

We rested while eying the rock wall directly in front of us. While the stream flowed on our left down a breathtaking waterfall, the same mammoth slab of granite which was the backbone to the waterfall rose straight up above us for forty feet. I was glad for the rest and glad for the view, but this was the first time all morning I took a serious glance toward the forest shelter and the trees that would offer me a safe way up and around the rock. I loved the thrill of the challenge. I longed for more, yet I also knew that I had little experience with rock climbing. A serious free climb up that face, with no net and nothing but granite to greet a fall, was not my idea of a challenge. Finally I had the good sense to recognize a dangerous climb when I saw it.

But I did not have the sense to suggest the forest option to Paul, who had been leading us upward. And Paul himself did not have the sense to see the danger in the climb. To him it must have looked easy, for he began the climb without a word. And like a lamb led to slaughter, I dutifully followed him up.

Actually, the climb proved easier than I expected. With Paul above me searching out the toeholds and fingering the rock for little handles of coarse texture, enough on which to pull our body weight upwards, I began to gain the confidence needed to complete the climb.

When I was about halfway up and Paul was close to the top, I saw him pause. Since he had not led me wrong all morning, I figured he just needed a bit of time to scope out the safest route. I climbed up a little closer in order to view his final move. Poised on a two-inch indentation in the rock wall, his right foot had a comfortable hold. But that was the only foothold, and the move to that hold looked complicated. I watched as he studied his next move. To my great dismay, he literally leapt out of his foothold, caught hold of two small branches from a tree above the top of the ledge, and pulled himself up over the top.

I stared at the vacant place where his body had been, uncertain if I had actually witnessed some miracle of levitation or if he was really that lucky. Just the absence of his company on that rock face left me feeling deserted, left my stomach a shrinking knot and my heart an empty space.

My mind went through a mechanical thought process. Willpower forced my hands and feet to move upward and brought me to the same place of Paul's decision. My right foot was in the same foothold he had used. My left foot dangled freely, occasionally grazing the vertical expanse of the smooth granite. My hands groped the rock longingly for places from which to pull the rest of me up. Since I was about four inches taller than Paul, I was sure I would reach a hold he had missed.

The top of the ledge was just above my head, but I could not see anything except the rock in front of me. Where I was perched, the ledge top was rounded and relatively smooth. In years past the water from the stream had done its work well, eroding all the small imperfections away—those same imperfections for which I was now desperately feeling. Now I understood why Paul had hesitated here. I too found nothing, not even a small nick or crevasse for a fingerhold.

I stole a glance down the thirty-five feet to the granite floor, and I knew that I could not reverse my moves and move downward without a fall. I was left alone there to think through the implications of serious injury, broken bones, and the terrifying flight down to a heap on a granite bed.

The fear of that vision gave me fresh determination to find a way up. I tried everything to find a grip on the top of that ledge; any intermediate move would have been worth a try. But once again I found nothing. I did not want to look at those two little branches Paul had used to pull himself up, but now I forced myself to see them again. I knew that I could reach them, but to do so meant I would have to leap out of my only foothold, my only hold on solid rock. I quickly turned away.

I tried to deny the fatigue in my right calf and thigh, and I succeeded until those muscles began to tremble. And then my entire right leg began to shake convulsively. I knew I was seconds away from a fall. So in absolute desperation I jumped for the branches, not even sure that I had the strength left to reach them.

A split second of hope flickered in my heart as my fingers closed around the branches, and then the branches both snapped, torn apart by my weight. I fell back, awaiting the embrace of air and the crushing end to the day's climb.

Attempting the climb had been a foolish thing. I had sensed it was beyond my ability. Pride had brought me to that last move, and with it my wish to keep up with Paul, my choice to forgo the safety of the woods. I was receiving my due, the consequence of a bad decision.

But then the most amazing thing happened. As I slid backward about eight inches, my right foot once again lodged in that familiar hold. I flattened my body against the rock and gasped for breath. A second chance—a lifetime—it seemed to offer me. That rock embrace supplanted all future lovers, gave me the momentary knowledge of wholeness. For that brief time I was saved, the rock my intimate pardon.

Yet still I was dangling by a thin thread. A two-inch pocket of rock and near exhaustion were precious little to postpone for long the real fall. Whatever Paul had been doing since he vanished over the top of the ledge, I needed him right then. I managed only a feeble call for help, partly because I really thought he had continued up the mountain. But no sooner had I blurted out his name than his head and hand reappeared from on top. He did not say a word—Paul never was one to waste effort on words—but in an instant he knowingly grabbed my wrist as we locked our arms together. He had been waiting there all along, ready to help when help was needed.

We only rested for a moment. I said thanks, and then we continued our upward climb. Perhaps three minutes of my life were spent on that foothold thirty-five feet off the granite bedrock, but I will always take with me the details of struggle—the certainty of the fall, the grace of a second chance, and Paul's hand reaching for me the moment I called. It wasn't God's hand, but it was close enough.

Some Angles of Justice

Justice is one of those English words that can be used in various ways, sometimes in ways unrelated to a serious understanding of well-being for humans and others. Part of the confusion over the meaning of justice has to do with our flippant way of turning a phrase or striking a motto.

On a recent trip to Washington, D.C., I toured the capitol building and the grounds around it. At the top of the building there is the statue of a woman. This lone female figure is said to be the statue of freedom. The eagle head and feathers on the crest of her helmet refer to the costume of the American Indian. Thoughts of the U.S. Congress creating a just society seem meaningless in the light of our nation's past story of sexism against women and genocide against Native Americans. Whenever justice rings out in word only, it is the lie that in the end defines the system and its decision makers.

Actually, the basic concept of justice flowing within our North American society clearly claims a lifestyle lived out only by those whose education, wealth, and sex qualifies them for this justice. Though the U.S. culture is underlined by a Christian mystique that is imprinted on our coins and in our political rhetoric, our concept of justice remains blatantly unbiblical. For God's justice sung by the prophets of the Old Testament and written in the life of Christ has little, if anything, to do with a bill of rights or the notion of equality or a concept of individual freedom or a maze of courtroom dramas meting out punishment.

When will we learn that justice is an attribute of God, a part of the One who brings all things to being? Justice is not about how people would structure their world. If so, then justice can never break free of our grasp. We will always depend on our wisdom serving only us all too well. Rather, justice originates with the Creator. We cannot create justice or bind it with human logic. Because we are creatures, we may choose to live justly within a just environment, but we do not dictate the rules for justice, just as we do not create the world. Ours is to live within a justly-created world, an order appointed by God. Justice by its divine nature has to do with how the world comes to be and how things exist naturally.

An easy conclusion drawn from my experience on the

rock wall might declare the injustice of my survival. I did not get what I deserved from   my choice and action. A fall resulting in great injury should have been the result of my error in judgment. Because of my pride, I deserved the fall. Others have come to great heartache and even death for lesser mistakes. Human logic would leave me at the mercy of the court of justice. The verdict would be "guilty."

Call it whatever you like—a great surprise, a shocking turn of events, undeserved and illogical—the fact that I didn't fall was due to gravity, the ageless shape of the rock, the limits of wood fiber, and my waning physical strength. There could have been no predicting the outcome of that climb, yet unexplainably I came to no harm.

God's justice as voiced in the biblical story is based on divine righteousness. Justice produces the hoped-for reality of people and the earthly environment living in harmony. Each receives its necessary nurture from the earth's resources. Each receives its necessary nurture from God's Spirit. Each is to live a dependent lifestyle, knowing that God sustains. God sets the agenda for the work of justice-making, which becomes the task of all whose needs have been met.

I am a white, middle-class male with all the privileges granted to me within our society. I did not deserve these privileges, and in a sense was born into them unjustly, if we look at it from our societal view. Like the undeserved outcome of my climb up the rock face, nothing I ever did earned me the advantages I enjoy. And though I will never understand all the mysteries of how God created a morally free world in which I live with the possibility of death and suffering and destruction, God's justice rings perfectly clear from the biblical story. If I am to walk in God's way of justice, then I must choose to execute justice for the oppressed, give food to the hungry, set the prisoners free, open the eyes of the blind, lift up those who are bowed down, watch over the strangers, and uphold the orphan and the widow. That, according to Psalm 146, is God's way in this world.

The Bible is not a bill of rights. The Bible is the story of God's way. The Bible is our call to realize the gift of life all around us, to see the grace of God's handhold over death. The Bible is our guide to living God's life here on earth. Each person must choose if they will live for themselves within a mystique of individual freedom, or if they will let go of their claim to freedom to serve others in need. And today "others in need" surely includes the suffering of the earth and all the creatures of the earth.

The bounty of an undestroyed earth gives witness to the bounty of God. The regenerative nature of creation cries out the potential of a world of justice. Creation itself claims the prize of justice. No, not a perfect world where none would need to make a moral decision, but a world full of the potential for right living. We decide. Will it be our justice or God's justice? The American dream has not brought God's justice on earth. The real question must reside with those who claim a biblical faith, who want to follow God's way, who believe that God spoke through the psalmist and the prophets, who believe Christ to be God showing us the way. Will these people choose their own justice or will they choose God's?

If indeed creation itself displays the justice of God—the results of God servicing the needs of life itself—then for people to hoard or use up or pollute the earth strikes an evil blow at God's reign. Part of the job of a biblical people is to clarify the meaning of justice, to restate the Bible's claim to its meaning, and to understand the universal implications literally for all created life. And from these understandings this biblical people must decide if they will be a faithful people.

Forests of Stone

I could tell a hundred tales of trash and destruction. Every time I travel the wilderness I see it. As if we need far places in the woods to take our things that will outlast the organic cycles of life, people spread their waste about like sprinkles of their worn-out hope for the world or their anger at a God who has not pleased them enough.

But these are not the stories of God and God's justice ecology. There lives and breaths in this world a much grander tale, a much more magnetic reality. It is a creation story, a recent event unfolding still on a grand scale right before our very eyes. For here in northeast Minnesota, as in places everywhere across our planet, God remains at work, breathing life into an otherwise crusted and barren land.

The forests of northeast Minnesota have blossomed to their present state within the last 11,000 years. This is but a moment in geological time. Yet when the last glaciers receded from the Wisconsin period of the Pleistocene Epoch, the winds and rains immediately began their work on the glacial deposits and the bare rock landscape. Reshaped and scarfed clean, the surface of the earth had been reborn.

Oh, to have had the opportunity to look out over such a vast genesis of earth and water, where almost every living thing was a future hope within the organic process! What would it have been like to walk upon the ground before the forests were born and to eye the now water-filled depths when they were empty, awaiting their fertility patiently. This was the scene then: while empires were rising and falling in warmer climates, no human breath was exhaled across the glistening waterways of the north.

But the flow of life could not be stopped by the glaciers. Once the average temperature rose a mere five degrees, the snows could accumulate no more through the summer months, and life returned from its wintery grave. Though no one knows the exact pace, life steadily developed.

Slowly, a carpet of soil began to cover much of the granite. The lakes began to harbor more and more complex forms of life, and the soil gave birth to seeds borne by the wind and destined to reforest the earth.

The great boreal forests (northern conifers, quaking aspen, and white birch) and the mixed forest (white and red pine, red maple, red ash, yellow birch, silver maple, and basswood) developed over thousands of years. As the forest environment developed and continued to deposit more soil, the diversity of animal life increased to include mice, chipmunks, moose, and black bears. Today these forests are still home to timber wolves, bald eagles, and lynx. And though the winters in the northwoods remain harsh, after 11,000 years there exists here an amazing diversity of life—a community of plants, animals, soil, rock, and water.

Within the space of 11,000 years life found genesis and abundance. The fertility of the environment itself speaks the word of creation. The necessities of all these living things are present, awaiting their use and reinvestment back to the soil. While it is not ours to look out over the fresh landscape of 11,000 years ago, it is ours to look out over the product of 11,000 years of creation. And ours is the question: Will we see the symbols of justice in every living thing? Can we see the coexistence, the cooperation, the mutual dependency, the natural ways that the soil develops and returns the nutrients to the lives of others? Can we patiently understand the way of creation justice, the way life was meant to blend together, and to nurse and nurture the growth of new life? Why, for the sake of earth and heaven, drawing our conclusions from the last 11,000 years of life's miracles here, could we even for a moment think that humanity could live by any other law than the law of nature, God's own justice, God's way of giving and sharing life?

Isaiah's Vision Once More

The window I stare through stares back at me with a vision of 11,000 years of reality, of life threaded together over time. A red pine towers above the scene. The window cannot contain it, it grows too tall. And though the light of day is waning, I can still see the tree trunk, speckled from top to bottom with patches of faint red bark. At seventy feet tall it may be but half grown, still filled with the vigor of a youth training for the marathon of existence. The red pine is both older and younger than I am, for I am not its age but still I am past my prime.

There are five white birch trees close beside the pine. They take their solace in numbers, I guess, since they cannot match its height. I see these five more clearly now as the light softens into dusk. Such a wonder they are, with their bold white flags flying against the darkening greens. They seem to cast off their excess white like wisps of hair gathered at the barber's feet. These white poles rise in a slender stretch to the sky within the forest canopy. And they grace the woods as if they were youth cheering on the rest of the forest foliage simply by their strength and desire.

The closest tree seems to have feathery wings instead of needles or leaves. This tree becomes a darkening arrow in the night, for it aims straight for the stars. It is a northern white cedar, a light-hearted tree with grain as straight as its trunk, and stiff, lightweight wood that floats in the heavy night air. The bark of this tree is as brown and stringy as the hair of a moose when it gets matted down its back and sides.

To the right of the red pine balsam fir are growing. With stiff, flattened needles they stick out their arms in all directions like a May pole flailing its steamers all on its own. A weak, pulpy wood lies beneath the surface of these friends, and they are no match for the power of the pine.

I can make out one, maybe two, white spruce growing

amid the smaller trees. If the soil is good and moisture and drainage are in balance, they will someday rival the pine for its lofty perch above the other trees, for their Maker has granted them the quest of the forest top. Just below and a short walk away there are two giant white spruce that testify to the truth of this lofty genetic brew.

Up on the ridge where drainage is poor, white pine and jack pine mix with aspen and alder. There are black ash in the marsh below with tamarack and more alder. All these trees and others carpet the landscape, blanket the hillsides, and grow in every available space. If the land is torn apart and the trees taken away, they will slowly return. If the scorching heat of a forest fire chars the woods black, the trees will return. If indeed we ever see a fifth sheet of glacial ice rasp its way across the land, the trees will return.

A 200-foot white pine growing out of soil perhaps three feet deep can only be seen as a miracle. And this is but the symbol and sign to all the miracles of life that encourage and sustain the forests of the North. Nowhere in human culture can we find community the likes of the northern forest. With its mass of intertwined roots and interwoven branches, it becomes one growing thing. The delicate balance of life has found shelter in its common life. Eleven thousand years is not too long to wait for such wholeness.

Once more I refer to Isaiah's vision (see Isaiah 11). We take this vision as a glorious future, perhaps the conclusion to life on this earth. We seek the distant time when we will live in a paradise of God's design. We want a controlled environment with the perfection of peace and tranquility. We want the universe to revolve around our vision of just reward and just punishment in which all get what they deserve.

But we have twisted Isaiah's vision by making it a future reality. We have put it out of reach and out of our responsibility. We have not understood that the vision's purpose was to enliven the faith of the living and not of the future dead.

If we could only see Isaiah's vision in the ground of the northland, in the trees and all they shadow on the forest floor. If only we could see his vision where the community of life holds council together in the birthing process that continually makes way for new life. While the wolf and the lamb may have not yet lain together in safety, most of creation lives this vision every day within plain view of all who would be willing to witness its wholeness and harmony. To rephrase Isaiah 11:9, the whole earth is full of the knowledge of God as the waters cover the sea.

We who would like to live in a world where we get what we think we deserve and therefore act accordingly, get in return a wooden God, the God of Pavlov's dog. With this view of God there is no future hope, for there is no real God and no life beyond determinism. If this is the justice we seek—the rewards of heaven for a life lived dutifully and punishment for the wrongs we do—then ultimately we have become our own god.

Yet we have another option, the vision of Isaiah, the truth of who God is and who we are meant to be. Justice is an act of grace, an act of God in righteousness judging the poor and deciding in equity for the meek of the earth (verse 4). Once again, we can decide to live our lives according to God's justice. Justice is a process in our imperfect world. It arises from the act of mercy. God's justice requires our hearts and hands to lift up the down-and-out, to relieve the suffering of those around us, to guard with delight the natural harmony and justice in the created world around us.

Taught by the model of creation, tutored by Scripture, driven unceasingly by God's Spirit—all those given strength and privilege in this life are called to bear the arms of God's justice. It is up to those who are able to call for God's justice, for there are so many who are unable and so many who cannot otherwise live. There is so much of creation that cannot otherwise withstand the assault of the human population. I must speak for myself, for I was granted a way up the rock wall of life, though I did not earn it.

I must speak for myself, for I am socially privileged, though I did not earn it. And in speaking for myself, I look to God's justice ecology for my words. I will mouth the story of the forest. My life will be rooted in shared soil. My heart will live among the branches of other trees. And my thoughts will grow slowly over the years to mature into soil that gives life to all things.

Blessed are . . .

    Blessed are the poor in spirit . . .
    Blessed are those that mourn . . .
    Blessed are the meek . . .
    Blessed are those who hunger and thirst for righteousness . . .
    Blessed are the merciful . . .
    Blessed are the pure in heart . . .
    Blessed are the peacemakers . . .
    Blessed are the persecuted . . .
    Blessed are the slandered . . .

Blessed are . . .

                Matthew 5:3-11
                author's paraphrase

Chapter 11

Living the Beatitudes

What was meant to be

In *Watership Down* (Avon Books, 1972), Richard Adams weaves a wonderful tale of mystery, danger, anticipation, and hope. The story is about rabbits—rabbits that seek their way in the world apart from convention and the expectations of others. The book begins as a small band of rabbits decide to leave their home because one of them, Fiver, has sensed a great danger for the home warren. And as this unlikely group of misfits ventures into the unknown of the woods and open meadows, streams, and hills, they encounter many threats from wild animals, the elements, and even other rabbits. But each time they are faced with the possible breakup of their little band, one thing seems to hold them together. When in trouble, they call upon Dandelion, their storyteller, to tell them a story.

The stories that Dandelion tells are about El Ahriarah, the mythical head and father of the entire rabbit community. It is one of these stories about El Ahriarah that I wish to reweave for you in the event that you, too, may feel the forces of the wide world threatening your existence. It goes like this....

One day in the early years of the world before the animals had all of their distinctive features, Frith, the god of the animal world, decided to call the heads of the animal communities together for a meeting. It was Frith's plan to give each different animal a special gift, to bless them in a way that would set them apart from all the other species. Frith was a good god who cared about each of the animals and looked out for them.

But when the day and time of the meeting arrived, one animal was missing. El Ahriarah, the head of the rabbit community, was nowhere to be found. You see, El Ahriarah was a mischievous rabbit with a strong will of his own. El Ahriarah liked to party and have fun, and meetings called by Frith were not always high on his list of priorities. So it turned out that while the other animal species were being given their special gifts, El Ahriarah was out enjoying himself, heedless of the great changes taking place in the world.

What El Ahriarah did not know was how great a danger he and all his community were now facing. For he did not know that Frith gave the fox sharp teeth and a hunger for rabbits. He did not know that Frith gave the cat sharp claws and a hunger for rabbits. He did not know that Frith gave the dog a loud bark that would send any rabbit into shock at its very sound. He did not know that now he and all his community had a thousand enemies waiting for the chance to catch them and eat them.

The story of the animals receiving their gifts could have turned out very badly for all the rabbits. But remember, Frith was a good god who looked out for the animals, and Frith cared for El Ahriarah despite his mischievous ways. Frith knew that El Ahriarah had missed the meeting, so

Frith went to look for El Ahriarah.

Even as Frith set out to find him, El Ahriarah knew that he had done wrong by missing the meeting, and perhaps he was afraid that Frith would come looking for him. El Ahriarah was on the lookout for Frith and happened to see Frith from a distance coming down the path toward him. Rather than face Frith and receive what El Ahriarah thought would be punishment, he ran to the side of a near-by hill and began to hurriedly dig himself a hole in which to hide.

But Frith came down the pathway a bit too quickly and spied El Ahriarah, even as half of him was still out of the hole. Now perhaps Frith liked El Ahriarah because Frith too was a bit mischievous. For Frith, upon seeing half of El Ahriarah protruding from the hole, decided to bless what he could see.

It would be so simple to draw our conclusion from this story of Frith and El Ahriarah and say that this explains how rabbits got their strong hind legs and their fluffy white tails. This indeed is the conclusion drawn by Dandelion as he recounts the virtue of those speedy hind legs that make it possible for rabbits to survive the threat of being eaten by other animals. But perhaps there is a deeper moral to this story, one which also speaks to the human condition.

I was first introduced to *Watership Down* when I read Stanley Hauerwas's book, *Community of Character.* In fact, Hauerwas plays with the very same story of Frith and El Ahriarah, saying that the deeper moral lies in the knowledge that rabbits were never meant to control their world; they were not created to be a dominant species. Rabbits, in fact, were meant to live within a dangerous world and to do so by telling their stories, by relying on their speed and wit, and by depending on one another's gifts.

The writer of Matthew tells us that Jesus gathered his disciples on a mountainside in order to teach them. It was the beginning of his ministry, a pivotal moment. Many questions had to be running through his mind; this event would set the course of his years with them. What could possibly form the foundation of his future instruction? How could he say some of the tough things he had to say? How could he confront the major issues of obedience and discipleship? His choice was simple. He began by blessing them and at the same time describing them, telling them who they were. He began with the beatitudes.

> Blessed are the poor in spirit...
> Blessed are those who mourn...
> Blessed are the meek...
> Blessed are those who hunger and thirst for
>   righteousness...
>
> Blessed are the merciful...
> Blessed are the pure in heart...
> Blessed are the peacemakers...
> Blessed are those who are persecuted for
>   righteousness sake...
> Blessed are you when people revile you and
>   persecute you and utter all kinds of evil against
>   you falsely on my account...
>   (Matthew 5:3-11)

Jesus was not speaking to separate groups of people. He wasn't saying that those over in the corner are blessed for being poor in spirit; those in the back are blessed for mourning; those in the middle on the right are blessed for being meek. No, he spoke directly to his close followers as one group, saying, this is who you are and this is a blessing!

In Hebrew thought and family life the idea of blessing was an important one. Perhaps we can get a better understanding of this if we look briefly at the tradition of birthright in the Old Testament. Remember the struggle between Jacob and Esau? Remember why we typically say Jacob's name first, even though he was the second son? Remember the way it tore their family apart for so many years? The birthright blessing was special. It set the pathway for the stability of family life, its future, and its fortune. Blessing, therefore, was personal. It confirmed a personal relationship between generations, and it was meant to keep the family traditions and welfare strong.

With the beatitudes Jesus is saying, this is what it is like to be in my family, this is the birthright given to all sons and daughters of God, this is what keeps us together over the generations. Happy are those who live as peacemakers, who mourn over the state of the world, who know the limits of their spirituality, who live meekly like Moses—a meek man, but still a great leader. Happy are those who... Blessed are those who...

Oh, for Christians to understand that the beatitudes describe their lives! These blessings by Jesus in Matthew 5 confirm the very nature of those who are the salt of the earth and the light of the world (Matthew 5:13-14). We so often look at our lowly state or at our limited power and think of this more as a curse than a blessing. But Jesus says just the opposite, he turns the tables on us and defines a new sense of being God's children.

The only real question is this: Can we envision ourselves as the poor in spirit, the meek, those who mourn, those who hunger and thirst for righteousness, those who make peace, those who suffer persecution and slander for the sake of God, those who are pure in heart, those who are merciful? Will we accept the blessings of Jesus? Will we allow our self-identity to be these things?

Only when we have come to terms with the beatitudes in this way and are willing to claim them as the truest truth about our lives, and only when we are willing to commit to primarily identifying ourselves by Christ's blessings, will his teachings fully make sense as applied to our daily lives. The beatitudes script the remainder of the Sermon on the Mount. And for that matter, they script Christ's life and teachings in the Gospels. Think of some of the tough teachings of Jesus: loving enemies, praying for persecutors, lust as equal to adultery, turning the other cheek, not storing up treasures on earth, not judging. Too often these sayings are dismissed as teachings that were not intended for our day-to-day living. But if we feel, deep in our hearts, that our true selves are flooded with the sensation of being the blessed ones, and if we know conclusively in our minds that we are those described by the beatitudes, then Jesus' tough sayings would make perfect sense for us today. The key question remains: How do we identify ourselves? What criteria do we use to view ourselves? What shapes our self-appraisal, our self-esteem, our feelings of self-love or self-hate?

Feelings and thoughts about self are powerful motivators. One only has to scan television commercials to be reminded of the billions of dollars spent annually in order to take advantage of our need to feel good about ourselves. Big business knows how to get to our money, and they do it by capitalizing on our self-identity needs. Let us understand that we have options—important options—as to who and what sets the agenda for our self-worth and so too our motivation for living.

The beatitudes are more than simple statements held within a passive sense of the present. They are life-giving challenges to active living, for each one assumes a deep involvement with the world. The blessings are for those people who live as who they are, making peace, mourning over wrongdoing. The blessed ones are those who spiritually depend on God. The blessed ones are those living for God in ways that bring them persecution. The blessed ones are those who live out their meekness, who live according to their pure hearts, who hunger and thirst for righteousness in all that they do. But all the doing and all the living will remain undone without the vision. Without a solid sense of identity we flounder. Without a solid sense of identity we ebb away into society's mold. Without a solid sense of identity we water down the principles meant to guide our lives.

We live by a vision whether we realize it or not. Something motivates us whether we think about it or not. Often our motivation is to be in control, to work life to our best advantage, to use whatever resources of the earth that we can get, and to protect ourselves and our lifestyles at all costs. If this latter vision shapes our identity, little of what Jesus has to say will make sense. Even the beatitudes themselves will seem ridiculous. Is it any wonder then that over the past two centuries these sayings of Jesus have been interpreted right out of our present lives by so many well-meaning Christians?

Perhaps people and rabbits have more in common than first glance would indicate. Perhaps people were also never meant to control their world, but rather, to live in a dangerous world dependent on their gifts—their blessings, their wit and speed, their community, and most of all, the biblical story that tells them who they are.

Wilderness Wind

For the last seven summers I have lived in the north-woods of northeastern Minnesota, directing a wilderness canoe camp. These seven summers have brought me every emotion. With every tear and every feeling of satisfaction have come multiplications of both. The work begins at the end of May and continues nonstop until August greets September. Every August I am too weary to enjoy life and too drained to give life within relationship to others. At those tired times I battle depression and strained family relationships. I cease to care much about what I normally care about deeply. I move into a survival mode, and I promise myself that I will never again let my work get so out of control.

Those brave souls who take on the summer challenge with me are also tired come August, dead tired. They are voluntary service workers, understaffed and underpaid. They receive far too little thanks and praise for the terrific job they do.

I know these things well, for it is August while I write this chapter. So why do we operate Wilderness Wind, this summer base camp of hard work? We get little if any recognition. We lose valuable time from our regular occupations and careers. On some folks' scale of personal gain we would ride the minus column. Sometimes we too feel the ride dips into the negative numbers.

The answer I want to give and the answer you probably want to hear is that we operate Wilderness Wind because we are meek, pure in heart, and poor in spirit. Sorry, wrong answer. Life simply is not that easy to figure out.

Let me take another stab at it. We live here surrounded by the vast forest described in Chapter 10. We spend much of our time paddling canoes across a seemingly endless waterway of wilderness lakes and streams. We take our days, rain or shine, vulnerable to all the weather the skies might bring. Each night, perched on the water's edge, we greet the dark heavens coated with the speckles from a universal glitter box opened end for end. We become totally immersed in the experience of creation. It may be that we are swallowed whole. On wilderness evenings I sometimes feel that I will never be a person again with thoughts of myself, thoughts of my pride, thoughts of my wealth, or thoughts of my fears. I become bigger by gross calculation, and at the same time, I become small to the point of nothing. My life takes on a perspective that is mystery. I am enchanted by my glance with eternity, and I listen with an outside attention to the beat of my own heart.

The woods, the water, and the sky become real elements of my own nature. I do not want to be just a person again, just an individual with needs and wants of my own. What I want is to be transparent so the sky will shine through me and the water will wet me through and through. The significance of my existence rests with these elements of the Creator, and I am transformed by the renewal of my mind, my spirit, my body, my emotions.

This is blessing, a living glorious beatitude spoken by my Creator so that I may have new life. I indeed am the recipient of blessing, like the disciples on the mount overlooking the Galilean sea. Because of God's love and beauty flushing from creation like the joy of flowers in the spring, my spirit becomes calm; I am open to receiving more of God's blessings. These moments with God, within the artwork of God, allow me the space and time and mood to reassess myself. Because of the power in the experience, I am able to reach inside, opening deeper levels of self to God. The truth found in the beatitudes of Jesus strikes new chords of response in my soul. The beatitudes are who I am at my deepest level. And though I may not always know it or act it, the truth has been revealed to me.

God, who is the creator of all things, speaks in Matthew 5 for the way we are to be and to live. The Creator of all the glorious wonders of nature also sets forth the guidelines for the created. The beatitudes, the ideal reality of human existence, fit hand in glove with God's justice ecology. The world is one. The Creator has made it so. We, like all the other creatures of the earth, have been formed and fashioned to live as one with the earth and its community of life. Thus, the beatitudes of Jesus tell us who we are within not only the human community, but they also tell us who we are within the community of all life. Therefore, being poor in spirit, pure in heart, meek, and so on, directs our way of living within our creation environment. If we are to be the blessed of Christ's family, disciples of God's way, and proclaimers of God's reign, then the welfare of all living things and all the earth becomes our mission.

It makes no sense to glorify the work done here at Wilderness Wind. But I do think it safe to say that we endure the difficult times because we see a larger reality, a greater vision than our own small personal world. We hope to act faithfully from a deeper insight than personal struggle. And we hope to see the similar effects God's creation can have on other people willing to open themselves to God's blessings.

Vision and Reality

To claim a vision is one thing. To live it is another. Fortunately we have both in the Gospel narratives. The one doing the blessing is the one who is blessed. Jesus lived his own life on earth as an example of living the beatitudes. Many books have been written on Jesus' life and teachings, and I do not plan to add another to that long list. But I do think it is important to mention some of the connections here with the larger theme of this book.

Without going into great theological discourse on his nature, we should recognize the importance of Jesus as God incarnate. It would be good for anyone who claims the Christian faith to think about the implications of God coming to dwell on earth, to remove whatever barriers or distance there might have been. God is the God of this world, having experienced it in human form, having committed to the very air and water and soil from which we live. As John's Gospel states, "For God so loved the world, that [God] gave [us] the only [divine] son, so that everyone who believes in him may not perish but may have eternal life" (John 3:16). While through hundreds of years of interpretation of this text most Christians have assumed a strictly human meaning for the word *world*, it is high time to correct this biased view. The Greek word is *cosmos* and it is translated *world* because that is what it means. The cosmos is the entire world, or even the universe. The writer of John here makes a clear statement, completely in line with the opening text of John 1:1-3: that Christ's mission on earth has to do with God's love for the earth, all the earth. Salvation—as we have it at the expense of God's own son—has to do with God's care for the earth. Christian evangelists should chew on this awhile. Environmental concern should be anything but a secular concern, and it should be part and parcel of our salvation story.

It is Paul, the New Testament theologian, who says in Colossians 1:20, "Through him [Christ] God was pleased to reconcile to God all things, whether on earth or in heaven, by making peace through the blood of his cross." Paul also says in 1 Corinthians 8:6 that there is one God from whom all things come and one Christ from whom all things come. Speaking of Jesus Christ, the writer of the book of Hebrews claims that he is heir of all things, he created the world, and he sustains all things by his powerful word (Hebrews 1:2-3).

These statements of reconciling by the cross, of creating and sustaining all things—these are salvation language. In Romans 8 Paul says that creation itself is waiting to be set free from the bondage of decay so that it may gain the freedom of the glory of God's children. Humanity's reconciliation and salvation are linked to the reconciliation and salvation of all things. So there we have it. Scripture tells us that God created our world, came to dwell in it, and is reconciling it through the cross.

God incarnate carries the meaning and purpose of God's care for all creatures great and small. Even the life-giving environment cannot hide from its Creator's love.

We should not be surprised to find the many connections

that Christ's life had with the earth. In fact, the creation theme gives us a whole new slant on Christ's life and teachings. This theme can help to correct some of the anthropomorphic bias previously read into Scripture. In speaking of living the beatitudes, it is not incidental that Jesus was born in a stable (or cave actually) that sheltered various animals. Of all the lowly places for the ruler of the universe to enter this place called earth! Once again, this makes no sense unless we think like the beatitudes, unless we listen carefully to what Jesus has to say to us. Birthed and buried in a cave, the divine human from Galilee had intimate connections with even the crust of the earth itself.

We are told that Jesus was a carpenter by trade, so we know that in his early life he worked closely with wood and stone. He dirtied and soiled his hands on the raw materials of the earth. He was baptized in the muddy waters of the Jordan River. He then wandered alone in the desert wilderness wrestling with the devil and his own sense of self and mission. Time spent alone in natural settings was significant for Jesus. Counting the number of times that the Gospels report his need to pray in these places is important, but if we add this to the frequent times he left those places ready to approach a new challenge or to make a new decision, his time spent alone with God and nature seems to be an even more essential part of his life.

We know that Jesus spent much of his time outdoors traveling about the countryside, teaching the people wherever he went. Consider the number of stories in the Gospels that place Jesus on a mountainside, on the Sea of Galilee, in a lonely place, feeding the crowds, stopping to talk to people on his journeys. Think of the stories of Jesus eating meals with people. Always these times are spent in other people's houses, for Jesus was homeless as we noted in Chapter 2. Think of all the parables and other teachings of Jesus which take their basic lessons from the soil, or from the fruit trees, or from the many other objects of nature.

It reminds me of the vast difference between the farmer and the city dweller. One typically lives so close to the land that it is a part of them, and the other typically lives so far from the land that they are alienated from any sense of oneness with the soil. Jesus spent his life close to the earth, to the wind and rain and dirt. His life would have been much like the farmer in that he did not have to preach his oneness with the earth because he lived it. Jesus walked humbly with God, walked humbly with humanity, and walked humbly with the earth. The story of his life is the reality of living the beatitudes with all of life.

Destination: Payne Lake

A week-long canoe trip can be a miniature slice of life. Though the location, the geography, and the tasks of life are different, much of life's challenge and process remain. This becomes especially true when traveling with a group.

Last July I again headed into the Quetico Provincial Park in Ontario with a group of seven others. We were paddling four canoes loaded with provisions for seven days. For our entry point we were routed through Kawshipiwi Lake, which meant that we were headed directly into the heart of that wilderness area. Kawshipiwi is not one of the easier routes into the Quetico because of the number and length of the portage trails one must cross to get there. I knew this as I worked with the others planning the trip because I had been through the area before, albeit many years ago. Ten years shaves a lot off the edge of one's memory.

We began our journey early in the morning while the sun was still low along the eastern horizon. Fortune was with us as the breeze blew steadily from the southwest, speeding us on our way. The taste of the morning was crisp and fresh, tantalizingly spiced by the clip of the wind blowing over our left shoulders. Every time I begin a canoe trip on a clear morning I mentally cherish the good-byes to civilization. I liken it to unloading, one by one, the burdens carried over the previous months. With every paddle stroke I let the knot slip a bit, at every lap of water against the canoe I awaken ever so slightly. My sleep, you see, and my burdens accumulate with the amount of my distance from wave patterns on wilderness lakes, from shorelines that jog and angle and ripple in their own fashion up into passages begging to be explored.

So our passage northward led us into the awakening jungles, plains of wild grasslands, safaris of exuberance with calibrated firearms and sights raised to the brow. We took our aim. Kashipiwi would bow to the bullet's blow by the second nightfall.

The morning was grand and equaled our anticipation. Then we turned west along the border and met the wind straight up and flat into our faces. The canoes began to make a furrow deep into the never-ending waves, a furrow that laid aside angry water and collapsed behind the boats in a rush like the divine judgment on Egyptian folly at the Red Sea. Our passage into the northern lakes suddenly became hard work. We braced our feet and knees against the canoe sides, set our paddles deep with each stroke, and chose to meet our first physical challenge of the trip.

Sucker Lake was actually only the beginning of the westerly wind that was turning northerly even as our route did the same. Inlet Bay and Bayley Bay of Basswood Lake became increasingly rough. Lunchtime found us on the portage to Burke Lake, tired and longing for the wind to cease. But when Burke greeted us with a blast of wind out of the north strong enough to blow our hats off, we knew the afternoon's job would be even more taxing. That northerly was kicking up whitecaps all over Burke, and they were piling up almost at our feet. Lunchtime was spent squinting into a water-darkened roller coaster with foam riders waving at us in sinister delight.

We wanted to linger over the last bites of bread and cheese, maybe take an extra day to wait out the wind. But our sights were still set further into the woods and water. So we loaded the canoes and pulled hard into the wind. By midafternoon we were on North Bay of Basswood Lake, heading due north toward South Lake. The wind was even worse there as we rode out the waves marching into us from the north and the west, since the sprawling body of the lake channeled the wind from this split direction.

I could have enjoyed the ride if I had not been so concerned about how the others were holding out. What was intended as a moderate day of easing our group into the wiles of wilderness canoeing had become a day of intense labor. By late afternoon we pulled into a campsite protected from the wind on the far northeast edge of North Bay. Because of the wind we had not made the distance we hoped to that first day. We finally relaxed and caught our breath, while I wondered about the labor the next morning would bring us. I knew the number and length of the portages that we would take one at a time. And if we made it into Kawshipiwi for our second night, we would be even more exhausted. I watched as the group reached for any physical reserve that would enable them to set up camp. Slowly, each person came back to life and joined in the business of setting tents, hanging food, and gathering firewood. And as each one contributed to the project, they also came together as a group of friends, cheering each other up and laughing about the difficulties of the day.

As the wind finally began to calm down, the evening became the perfect image of wilderness travel. The sun was setting over the lake. A pair of loons sang to us just offshore. The old saying, "All's well that ends well," began to take on renewed meaning.

Day two began gloriously with a calm lake and a bright

sky. We glided through the first several lakes and skipped over the short portages between them. We took our morning gorp break on Shade Lake while feasting on the beauty all around us. To that point the day could not have been more perfect and even I began to relax about the journey ahead.

Trouble slowly mounted as we searched for the portage trail out of Shade Lake. We knew we were in an area of the Quetico traveled less frequently than other routes, so we were not too surprised to have to search for the trail. But still, after paddling right by it and hunting for perhaps twenty minutes, we lost valuable time. Once found, the trail to the next lake—unnamed on our maps—was long and narrow. After roughly two minutes of paddling on that unnamed lake we were back to portaging again, this time headed toward Grey Lake. Here our real trouble began. We started the portage on a little-used trail, trudging uphill in dense forest. We did not know that our maps showed an old, seldom used trail, rather than a new trail. We found logs over the trail and precious few signs that the Canadian Forest Service trail crews had ever discovered the place. About ten minutes of fighting the close-growing bushes and the downed trees brought us straight into a large bog. Others had tried to walk through it, leaving what looked like a trail. But twenty yards into it I realized I was no longer on a trail. I set my canoe and pack down and backtracked until I found what looked to be the real trail skirting the bog off to the left. I ran down that trail for about fifty yards just to make sure it was not another dead end. This time it was the real thing, and so while my canoe was still back in the muck, I directed traffic around the bog. I then returned for my canoe and pack, loaded up, and followed the others.

By then I thought the worst was over, that we would follow the trail around the bog and be on our way. But another five minutes up the trail I caught up with some of our group heading up a different trail that could only take them in the opposite direction of the next lake. Once again I set down my canoe and pack to study the situation. This time I saw a clear trail leading through the bog and up the next hill toward Grey Lake. I could see why others were unsure of it since there was just about no way to carry a canoe across it without slipping into waist-deep water and muck. The trail that some of our group had taken was dry, clear of trees, and an enticing walk—in the wrong direction. So I jogged up that trail, hoping to catch up with them and turn them around. I finally caught up with the last member of our group who had already unloaded equipment at a lake—the same lake from which we had just come. At least we now had discovered the correct trail, which was not marked on either of our maps.

After finally crossing the bog (with no casualties) and finding Grey Lake, we stopped on a small island for lunch. By now one of our members was seriously sick to his stomach. And halfway through lunch another member broke off a large piece of his tooth on a fragment of a pit lodged in a dried peach half. The day was rapidly progressing from difficult to terrible. Each one of us struggled to make the best of it, believing that soon things would improve.

Wrong again. The second and last portage of the afternoon led from Yum Yum Lake to Kashipiwi Lake. I had traveled that portage ten years earlier, and I knew it would be a long one. What I did not remember was the steepness and ruggedness of the trail. Ten years before I had been traveling in the opposite direction, which meant that I had traveled downhill over the worst section of the trail. That day in July we were hot, tired, discouraged, and already in pain. Though we did not know it, we were not ready emotionally or physically for what would be the toughest challenge of our trip.

Yum Yum portage is not the longest portage trail that I have traveled, not even close. But it stretches for most of a mile up and down, over several steep rock ledges, through at least one small bog, and then plunges steeply to the banks of Kashipiwi. It would be a great hiking trail without carrying a canoe across it. But we had canoes and heavy packs, and the day had already held just about all the stress we could handle. Yum Yum portage that afternoon became a trip into mindless, numbing pain. We gutted it out because we had to.

With sweat-soaked shirts, shoulders in agony, and worn-out spirits, we dumped our gear at the end of the trail and pinched ourselves to be sure we were nestled up against the gentle flanks of Kashipiwi Lake. Slowly we loaded canoes and paddled to a beautiful island campsite about a mile up the lake. At the campsite everyone worked together to set up our night's lodging.

After two days of unplanned strain, we sat around the supper fire that night, determined to make our third day less stressful. The next morning we again poured over the maps and shortened our route by about ten miles over the next few days. We took that third morning out in lazy fashion, fully expecting the day to find us sunning on a gentle sloping rock by lunchtime.

Well, as you may guess from the way our luck was going, we were still in the canoes at lunchtime. And though we had made it to the lake where we planned to stay, we found absolutely no place to camp. Hurlburt Lake is long and narrow, so we scanned the shoreline on both sides, desperate for an afternoon of ease. But after an hour of searching, we moved onto the next lake and found nothing suitable for a group of eight people on that lake either. We pushed on to Payne Lake, where we again searched for close to an hour for a campsite. And just as I was conceding to the necessity of heading to Williams Lake, we spotted a possible site on a small island in Ahsin Bay. I had dismissed it earlier as a possibility because of its small size. But though the bathroom facilities would have to be on the mainland, that island was an almost ideal campsite. Finally we could settle down and rest our trail-weary bodies. Even that third day had become long and stressful with the seemingly neverending search for a campsite.

Amidst the tumult of those first three days while we were getting acquainted, any one of the members of our group could have declared the trip a bust. They could have let the stress erode any peacefulness of mind that might come from their experience of the northwoods. They could have turned their troubles onto the others in the group. And we could have been at each others' throats. In fact, I often wondered during those days why that did not happen. Even with all the careful planning that went into the trip, each member of our party had been physically and emotionally pushed beyond what they thought they could take. And the whole experience was not supposed to have turned out that way.

They probably would never have identified themselves as blessed. And they surely would not have pictured themselves similarly to those motley followers of Jesus hearing for the first time the true meaning of blessing. But our group of castaways, left to find our way through the Canadian woods, certainly lived out those beatitudes. Those first three days were anything but easy, anything but ideal, anything but comfortable, and anything but predictable. We had left our middle-class lifestyles behind, and for at least a time, we were taken into a third-class mode of survival. And it was within this real test that these people became the ones whom Christ identified in Matthew 5.

Without real-life adversity, real-life pain, and real-life struggle, how can there be a real-life choice to seek Christ's way? There simply is no choice for the one who already has it all. For we must see that Jesus was speaking to real people with real problems not very different from the problems facing our world today. If indeed our vision for life is the good life, the abundant life, the lifestyles of the rich and famous, so to speak, then even though we may never realize our dream, we have been defined by it and we follow it instead of Christ. For Christ lays out for us a clearly down-to-earth, salty vision of life's reality. And there amidst the dirt and the pain of life we find ourselves facing moral choices of the utmost importance. And as a people together, we can choose a oneness with Christ, and we can experience Christ's blessings firsthand, body and soul.

The Creator of the universe remains within sight and sound of our every move on this planet earth. If we know who we are meant to be, then we will end our search for God. For we will know God's presence in all the beauty and in all the pain. We will know God, for we will be living God's beatitudes.

The heavens are telling the glory of God,
  The sky proclaims God's handiwork.

Day to day pours forth speech,
    Night to night declares knowledge.
Without speech, without words,
    Their voice travels to all the world.
As the twenty-four hour journey of the sun,
    Their voice travels, Nothing is hid from its heat.

Yesterday the heavens told the glory of God.
Today the heavens are telling the glory of God.
Tomorrow the heavens will tell the glory of God.

                    Psalm 19:1-6
                    author's paraphrase

Chapter 12

Return to Belonging

Circle of Wholeness

Maybe the only thing new about the recent recycling craze is our long overdue attention to what has always been nature's way. It is late September as I write this, and the northwoods will soon take on the silence of winter. The cold brings a refreshing feel to the land, a familiar kiss of crystalline mornings. All of nature lives and breathes as a revolving doorway within the seasons. So how can it be that humanity seems to ignore the essential goodness of the cycle of life? How can we so often define life in ways that are not circular, when all around us life gives testimony to fundamental return. What leaves us returns to us, what dies away sprouts once more.

Even we, who attempt to find immortality within our self-worth, we live and die within the cycle. We do not gain a thing by all our attempts to step out of the circle. Dust to dust and ashes to ashes indeed. The biblical story has

223

always tried to deal honestly with this fact of human mortality. Though we are the crown of creation, we are but grass that withers away and is gone. And though in death we fashion cement boxes to slow the composting of our flesh, we can only postpone it and not prevent it.

What happens in the cycle of life illustrates a healthy wholeness, a natural healing, a continuous process without end or interruption. Even death only represents a phase in the cycle and therefore claims no final hold or passing. If we wish to feel a true sense of home within the natural world, then we must come to terms with the cycle of life. We must accept our own natural place within that cycle. We must accept that the cycle of life is fashioned by God and therefore overflows with goodness. We must touch it, press against it, lie within it, and submit our minds and bodies to it. Our encounter with the circle of wholeness created by God cannot be a simple logical thought based on data and deductions. Rather, any significant contact with the cycle will draw us into its movement; spirituality then becomes a whole body process, renewing every fiber of being.

Lest this sound far out and intangible, let me say that we people are impacted by our environment all the time. This is normal and as natural as breathing air. We all enjoy certain beauties of this world, like sunsets and rainbows, fresh green grass and flowing streams. But most of us have never learned how to trust this intimate invitation. Somewhere within all our layers of culture and civilization we have lost the hope of the land. The return of cyclical things cannot involve us with its passion. We have fallen prey to secularism on its grandest scale, for natural life no longer holds us in God's womb. We have asked for an unnatural birth and a separation.

What appears to be the worst separation of all comes in the form of a biblical people unable to connect with a significant theology and spirituality of the earth and of God as creator. And when we lose this connection between a biblically-based faith and the God of creation, then we risk all kinds of fragmentation among the Christian family. One of the best examples of this fragmentation arises from the so-called New Age movement and the alarm over it that is being sounded by certain evangelical Christians. Wherever I have heard this alarm, people have projected the heresy onto the New Agers without any self-examination concerning the cause of the problem. It saddens me to have to admit that the New Age movement gets its fuel from the deficient biblical faith and teaching coming from so many Christian churches. In an age when the environment itself is at serious risk and while people flounder for faithful answers to real-life questions, much of Christian teaching simply says that Christ is the answer to all our personal problems. Just believe and praise Jesus.

Mainstream evangelical Christianity must shoulder a healthy dose of responsibility for spawning the very heresies it rails against. There is something intrinsically evil about an organism feeding on its young. It is out of a void of theological application to the real needs of our world today that many people are leaving Christianity either by route of nonbiblical faith or by simple boredom. If the Bible becomes a tool to dismiss the needs of either humanity or any element of creation, then the needs will be addressed elsewhere.

If the Christian church truly desires a witness with integrity to the New Agers, then the Christian church must openly proclaim a God-centered biblical interpretation that dashes all our hierarchical views of creation. In fact, a serious theocentric understanding of Scripture can never tolerate placing a human value on creatures and things created and owned only by God. The fundamental flaw of any hierarchical view of people and our relationships within creation is that in placing value we have replaced God with ourselves.

A far more wholesome, and I would argue more biblical, way of understanding, knowing, witnessing, and celebrating God's community of life can be found within the simple concept of belonging. This concept embraces the circle of wholeness and welcomes the human soul into relationships bounded only by God's value system. To belong means to feel the deep acceptance and gratitude of spirit for knowing a peace about self, for knowing God's immeasurable love mirrored by the earth, for release from the driven lifestyles of consumers teetering on the precipice of their self-fashioned pyramid of subjugation. Belonging simply means an absence of denial. It means lifting the shades to reveal the direct sunshine of God's presence. Belonging shatters any sense of self-aggrandizement. To belong means to feel totally right about how God has created me and totally relaxed from the need to create myself into something else. Belonging means that I am empty and ready to be filled: ready for new relations, eager to flower in any season, cleared for takeoff into horizons unbounded.

In order to belong, I must not possess, but I must be possessed. I must not hold, but I must be held. I must not want, but I must know that I am wanted. I must not search, but I must allow God to search for me. I must not call to God, but I must hear God calling me. I must exist to be hunted and captured by God, living for the very moment of union between seeker and empty soul.

If my life is encircled by God and all God is doing, then all my energies for chasing heresies are better spent in knowing the work of God within and around me.

Might it be possible for Christians to find the place where they belong? Could we actually enter the circle of wholeness, perhaps for the very first time? Could we do it within a biblical faith journey? Indeed, could Christ really be the ruler of all creation?

The Christian faith either is or is not comprehensive of all life. Jesus either fits here or he does not. I imagine no partial work of creation or salvation; therefore, I can only claim the circle of wholeness as God in Christ, at work loving matter into animated, joyful being.

And so the question must be reframed: Can Christian people hear the Spirit of God passing through them as a slender reed bending in the current of a stream, as an ice floe expanding across the surface of that same stream, and as the stem once again pushing itself imperceptibly above the similar waters of another spring day? Are we the bending reed, the icy movement, and the tender shoot? Do we know that God moves us in the way that all creation is moved? Have we enough faith to let ourselves become caught up within the circle, the wholeness, the most powerful spiritual movement of all time and place?

A Place of Belonging

Crab Lake still calls to me, and I await the time when I may return to its shores. The rock there still cushions me against all of life's hardships. The night air still rings around my vision of the planetary movement of dark shapes representing the trees, the waves, the patches of sky. My place of belonging still overwhelms me with a cavalcade of unending movement known to me as passionate nurture and vast security.

Crab Lake calls and moves in me now, for it is a timeless representation of God's enchanting ways—ways which hold me fast, ways which bind me. And in Crab Lake's grip of grace I lie down, falling in love again. I float away, weightless, journeying past each of my fears as I un-name them and strip them of all shape.

And God comes to me as a shaking joy—that Spirit of hovering, that One of flotation, that God-ness of inside-outside infusion. Thus my memory flashes with brilliant light as the searing brand of God's Spirit transforms it into liquid energy, breathing into me the eternal knowledge of creature identity.

Like a hard rain, the plans of my life seem to pour out of me and vaporize. The blessing of God's grace comes to me within the pouring out. Even as I acknowledge that internally I reside upon that ancient rock or sprawled against a pine's rutted bark, I experience God's gracious "welcome home" in my heart.

I have found the cure to the heartache of the people. No, the cure will have no hearing in our thinking and our doing, for it is our thinking and our doing that often take us further from belonging. Our cure will never come by way of our most diligently sought-after objective, because the cure is found in what we allow to enter our hearts, our souls. It can be found when we allow a remake of how we think, for this then becomes a new spiritual beginning that reattaches us to the core of life deep in the soil and in the forest of creation.

In God's Spirit we find the content for our life's empty space, and God's Spirit reforms us internally into the natural process of life. I am spiritually shaped by matter because God's presence comes in natural pathways.

In belonging, I have found the meaning of being alive in God's grace.

Without a Wilderness Home

Far too many people know little of life beyond human scope and control. We concentrate on our own accomplishments, and admire the products of our species. We are caught up in manipulations of matter; scientific endeavors to benefit the human race.

We mostly live without a wilderness home.

Wilderness throws us. We flee its challenge. We mask its ability to unsettle us. We leave no stone unturned as we yearn for a prize to call our own, to hold onto. Our identity comes from what we think we must have. But wilderness would deny us this pleasure.

How we could learn from the community of life from which we are left out! How we could discover true diversity of relationships more numerous than the shades of the rainbow! All we would need is to know that community grows in the absence of manipulation, that it is our mirror gaze that must be shattered, that controlling something ends a relationship. We might also discover that God lives in exactly those places where we have not draped our own image.

God can be seen where our shadow does not first fall. Home then may be defined as that place of shattered self-images and reconstructed relationships.

On Entering Wild Places

Wilderness lives in land and soul. Wilderness provides a way beyond the outline of our own image. Indeed, when we enter true wilderness we are also entered, tossed about from within, and created to reflect a more divine image than our own.

We groan with the struggle of the entering. We often miss the chance to find an opening out of self, because we are lovers of the familiar.

But still, to see a new land we must seek a new spirit. This then becomes a true exploration. Any number of unexpected things could happen to impact my senses and my soul. Tragedy and heartache, great discovery and celebration could come at any moment. And we are unprepared for the thousands of possibilities, no matter how prepared we think we are. The impact of the surprises within the landscape—within the twisting journey of the spirit—constitutes wilderness travel. These surprise experiences have the power to form us into different people from the inside out.

If we understand our journey into wilderness in this way, then the beginning becomes a commitment. And this commitment involves our willingness to come close enough to many new things in creation so that we will be impacted, even surprised by them. So in the beginning of our travel we have chosen relationship. We have elected to open ourselves to community and untold friendship possibilities.

This way of entering emulates God's way of entering, for God comes seeking relationship within this world. Finally, we have begun a process which overcomes the distance between us and creation. We are becoming present. We are becoming like God; we are being as God is in the world. And we are discovering ourselves as the lost image of God.

By entering wilderness in this way we accept a new union with the God who relishes the wonders of the universe. It is this new unity with God that multiplies the effect of wilderness on our spirit and our soul. By closing the gap between ourselves, creation, and God, entering becomes the ongoing event that breathes animation into life itself.

Living the Journey

A key understanding of entering is its continuation. We see the movement of entering patterned by the movement in all of creation. The spirit of creation never rests, always journeys, and always dances. Water displays openly the secrets of nature's movement as turbid or placid, but always changing.

We humans readily search for somewhere to settle down. Settling down within life's journey means that we settle into a deeper sense of being on the journey. If we wish to be a people of God rather than a people of self, then we must know that rest refreshes us for further travel. Rest is never the purpose of a lifestyle. So our stopping places are chosen judiciously according to their strategic advantage for continuing travel. This applies to travel within the wilderness of woods and water as well as the wilderness of heart and spirit.

And we discover while resting and moving that God too travels, changes, journeys, and marches on. God comes to us as both constant and ever new. Our journey becomes a journey with God, forming a partnership in exploration. We must resist the lure to package the experience, to seal up the book of faith, and to nail down God. The Bible never has been and never will be a book to hold God. No book can hold God down, even for a moment. But the Bible can tell people of faith where God has been and what that has looked like. The Bible is a book for the journey. We read it as a source of strength, a source of guidance, and a source of warning against the termination of journey. With the Bible in hand and heart, we explore the paths of life. When we seek God in undisclosed places, we ourselves become the story of faith.

Those who do not choose the journey, choose comfort as a cover for their fear of travel. The journey has great risks. We could lose our way, lose our faith, lose God. But these are risks we must take or faith soon dulls and becomes nothing more than a list of fundamental truths.

We see those for whom faith has become a list. They are wooden in all appearances, and they do not live truthfully, for their inner thoughts and deepest uncertainties are never explored or expressed. Without this exploration and full expression, God will never be fully incarnate in their lives.

Faith begins as we choose to enter life as journey.

Friendships Stored in Earthen Vessels

A wilderness journey flows freely with potential friends. Life's journey should be anything but lonely, for all of creation sings together a song of friendship. But if we wish to sing along with our sisters and brothers of the woodlands and meadows, then we must stop being the dominant voice. Our voice belongs in the choir, integrated into the symphony of sounds and led by the strong harmony of God's voice.

We humans generally have a problem with singing harmony. We lose our chance to relate in intimate voice with the choir because we often choose to judge the value of the other voices. We forget that it is not the business of a choir member to place value on others' contributions. We forget that only God assigns value to creation, and that only God knows the worth of songbirds and fishers, bears and sunlight on leaves.

Dare we use our faith story to keep us on top of some pyramid of life, singing out loudly from that perch an awful song of dissonance with the world about? We seem to want to center our faith story on us rather than God, and we do this by placing value on objects of creation according to how useful they are or might be to the human community.

But in this judgment process are we not undoing what God has done? Look at all the ways creation has and is being destroyed by our calculations and designs. We are not acting on behalf of creation or God, we are acting on behalf of ourselves. The flood story retold in Chapter 5 gives clarity about our need to step back from our measurements of life, our ladder of value, our dominance plan. I hope that we really might be able to yet find some of the friendships waiting for us. I hope that we will be able to see how, without these companions, every aspect of human life is diminished, but most of all our spirituality.

Simplifying the Adventure

A wilderness trip leading us into potential relationships does not begin with the first step onto a mountain trail, but with the setting of our priorities as we plan for the trip. And it becomes essential to the spirit of wilderness travel that we carefully place the emphasis of our planning on real meaning. From picking menus, to selecting equipment, to choosing dates, and to dreaming of the actual wilderness setting, we must place ourselves fully in the act of the journey. We can do this through the simple tasks of preparation. We can do this through knowing that meaning is altogether different from complexities and buying power. The simplicity of the preparations seals the fate of the journey to come. In fact, this is the journey already begun.

We live in a modern world of distractions. There are a thousand doorways for us to open and enter. With each of these doorways there comes a list of environmental problems, but still we wish for the choices. The current environmental crisis is first of all a spiritual crisis, for none of the thousand doorways will lead us to life's meaning.

Rather, meaning is found in single-mindedness, in the simple task, in the patient waiting for fish to bite at sunset. God is found in the simplicity of being present, when we sit at God's feet and listen to the music of our soul. And when we reach this simple spirituality, we also become present to other people and to all of creation.

The power of wilderness strips us of all the things we do not need so that we might clearly see the one thing that we do need. God joins us with generosity—with presence—to fill us full of spiritual being. This generosity can remake us into generous persons, not giving from our abundant choices, but giving of ourselves. As spiritual beings, we become communion for the earth and the creatures dwelling upon it.

And in this communion we no longer must search frantically for God. Surely we now may see God and hear God and touch God within the myriad expressions of life before us. We have become rich in a multiplicity of spiritual blessings, while remaining centered on a single presence, a single striving, a single God.

Healing the Human Spirit

Our human strivings have cost us a great price—the price of our spiritual health. Much of Christian life remains caught in the theological ramblings of self-sacrifice or blind praise. Both search for God among the rubble of human identity. We will be caught here forever until we stop idolizing our place among all God's creatures. As long as we keep trying to work our way or praise our way into God's loving embrace, we will never recognize the wonderful panorama of God's grace that exists outside human life. This panorama is poised to fully impact us and surround us in love.

What I have called natural piety brings us into an understanding of God that releases our grip on life. It is a theology fashioned within relationships of all kinds, and so becomes a living theology. Our understanding of God grows from the soil of all our encounters with creation, we know God because we are known within the world. This has everything to do with giving and receiving, mutuality, friendships of faithfulness, community accountability, and a combined and gathered worship celebration.

Wholeness can be found since our theology has been transformed. We are no longer seeking to heal ourselves, to bring ourselves to spiritual healing. We are willing to accept the impact of the theology that rules the order of the world and claims God's ready embrace. Yes, the healing of the human spirit can be as natural a process as melting snow or shining sun.

Servants of Natural Life

To live a natural piety would also mean that we could bring ourselves in honesty before the text of the Bible. Honesty can be painful, as when we must admit to our failure—of not living within the covenant of the Bible. Even so, we must become an honest people if ever we wish to live in harmony with the ecology of creation. And it will take a return to childlike anticipation and an eagerness to explore the text with abandon, to bring our lives into their proper context in this world. At their best, children search a new experience seemingly with no self-interest. They tackle a challenge with little thought of safety. They seem to have the ability to unlearn in the presence of truthful revelation.

We adults would do well to consider bringing that much openness to the biblical text. The passage in Mark 10 where Jesus speaks to the disciples about greatness would be an excellent place to start. But be forewarned that this means the loss of our old understandings about the world and our role in it. The text will challenge us and strike down any resistant hints of dominance or human judgment of creation.

In an unexaggerated way, Christ's teaching on greatness in Mark 10 forms a basic guide for Christian living. This text turns our thinking upside down. But I believe that Jesus meant it. This is the reality of who I am, of who we are meant to be. Taking my place as last in line, as the servant to all the earth and all the people of the earth, is my   inheritance in Christ. This took him to the cross. Today, this central Christian symbol is our harshest critic, for most of us have lived in any way possible, but not as servants last in line.

Jesus did live this way. He proved to us how radical and how possible this life could be. The world—not just the people of the world—continues to reel from the impact of his life. One life among the billions of human lives spent walking the earth has changed our reality and our purpose for living. By definition, Christians all over the world are called to life in service to the world. For we follow the servant God.

Nurtured in Nonviolence

Standing opposite to servanthood is violence. Violence has been understood by some Christians as a necessary evil, allowed for the betterment of the human race. This way of understanding the world, humanity, and even God, has been and continues to be possibly the worst evil to ever visit the earth. Violence is an attitude, an understanding of reality, a deep inner harbor for all the worst of the human soul. Violence remains ingrained in the fiber of our being, for we feed it there.

Human violence has the potential to finally kill all things. And so we have made the world dangerous, unsafe for the children of all creatures, including our own.

Within our encounters with the natural world lies a possible hope or a possible desperation. If indeed we can come to creation with openness, we may find that violence is not tended there. In the majority of locations within creation, we find the nutrients to feed our healing from violence.

Though Christians may be a violent people, we should realize that we own a faith story to the contrary. Christ, our creator and savior, brings as divine mission to this world a ministry of reconciliation for all things. Our story tells us this, and yet we seem to pay it no heed whenever we rationalize a need for violence. We forget that the Christian good news not only includes nonviolent teaching, but it culminates in an act of nonviolence. Our servant God has served us most supremely through the love of the cross. Here, awaiting our rediscovery, is direction for our life within this planet. Divine service—that greatness and firstness commended by Christ in Mark 10—becomes for us for all time the way of nonviolence.

While society at large may threaten to reshape us once again into its violent ways, the grand scale of creation counters with an even greater invitation. We may lap up the patience of a landscape and turn it into years of calm. We may look out over distances spanning centuries of ancient growth and be given rest from our frenzied search for control. Christians all over the world may, in light of our story, claim a new inclusive pacifism extended to the breadth of earth's ecosystem.

Finally then, as we rest within our faith story, we see Isaiah's vision of the lion lying down with the lamb. God has brought us together with all the earth at last.

God's Justice Ecology

Another way of speaking for God's way in this world is to speak of justice. Though there is often misunderstanding and debate over its meaning, Christian people know that God's justice carries far beyond our own notions of justice. Within the created order of things, within the various ecosystems of life on this planet, we see how living organisms of all varieties coexist and gain what they need to live. And the one who brings all these little and big things into being also structures the systems of life to provide the needs of life. So we also see that divine justice has to do with the very nature of life on this earth.

Justice—God's justice—has little to do with all the expectations of rights and freedoms in which we North Americans have come to believe. Rather, God's justice has everything to do with meeting the needs of people, animals, and all things. God's justice produces the hoped-for harmony of existence for all the earth's inhabitants.

Will we be a people of God's justice, or will we be a people of constitutional claims? The two worldviews are not compatible.

Wonderfully, the sustaining strength we need to be a people of God's justice can be found within a careful observation of natural life. But we must stop destroying the things that God has put here on earth to give life. It is Isaiah's vision again that can give us hope, for so much of natural life is all about living that vision. So much of natural life already lives in a harmony unmatched by the human community.

As one so privileged, living in a privileged society, I must ask myself the question of whether or not I will live justly so that others and other forms of life might live. I must choose my lifestyle according to justice, which is first and foremost understood biblically as an attribute of God. May I be granted the courage and the vision. May we be granted the courage and the vision.

Living the Beatitudes

The vision and the courage for living God's way in this world can be found in Matthew 5. The beatitudes form this vision that gives Christianity its calling and hope, and tells us who we are. The beatitudes also describe Christ's life as we see it spread out over the Gospel narratives.

This may not be what Christian people want to hear. The beatitudes do not describe the high and easy life. But the beatitudes do tell of a people who live in blessing because of who they are. The meek and the peacemakers, the poor in spirit, and the persecuted are Christ's devoted followers then and now. This life modeled after the lifestyles of the *not* rich and famous, is all about how one lives in harmony with all people and all the earth. Living in harmony flies directly in the face of a world torn apart, a world of people at war, a world bleeding the blood of the cross.

Living the beatitudes happens to be some of the greatest news of all time. This way of living brings meaning to all life's struggles because it both transcends and incorporates them within a way of being. It is a natural way of being. It is a humble way of being, without the trappings of dominance, hierarchy, and control. In fact, it offers our lives as sacrifice to the very powers that tout these trappings. If you do not like the thought of sacrifice to these powers, and if you are a Christian, then what are you doing following the very one who leads you to a cross?

The really great secret that Christ let out of the bag for all time is that in the reality of personal sacrifice, the powers are powerless. Suddenly we see the sham. We see that we do not have to live unjustly just because we are told it is the American dream.

Living the beatitudes closes any final gap which may yet have existed between the Christian and the environmentalist. For living the beatitudes puts us at one with all the persecuted of the earth's environment, at one with all the meek of the planet, at one with all the peacemakers bringing wholeness to the world, and at one with all who mourn the evils of violence and the attitudes of control.

Living the beatitudes puts us at one with God's journey here on earth.

Crab Lake

For all those people who have fallen prey to secularism's grandest hungering—the separation of the spiritual from the material and the separation of faith in God from the works of God—I invite you to a night with me upon the rock on Crab Lake's shore. We will wonder together how our vision of reality ever became so twisted. Out of silliness we will try to count the stars twinkling overhead. We will agonize over the pain the earth must bear due to human want and destruction while we poke the fire and guess the distance to where the loon calls to us.

Laughing and crying, we will go through the night encircled and encircling one another with emotion and vision.

As for me, I will wish my last night on this earth to be there on that same rock. My business there will again be to encircle you with my friendship, which is in turn encircled by the friendship of the earth, which is in turn encircled by the friendship of God. There I will die within the sacred cycle of life. But our friendship and the new vision that we share will live on.

My last thought for you is the hope that by now you know that the Gatekeeper, God, will always allow your passage into a wilderness home.

About the Author

Tim Lehman, an ordained minister, serves as co-pastor of Faith Mennonite Church in Minneapolis, Minnesota. During the summer, along with his pastoral duties, Tim directs a wilderness camping program, Wilderness Wind from a base camp near Ely, Minnesota, which sends canoe trips into the Boundary Waters Canoe Area of Minnesota and into the Quetico Provincial Park of Ontario.

As part of the Creation Care Mennonite Voluntary Service Unit, Tim writes and speaks on the topic of the Bible and creation. He is active in Mennonite Camping Association, and currently serves as president-elect.

Previous to moving to Minnesota, he lived and worked for nine years in central Kansas. Much of that time he was associate pastor at Eden Mennonite Church, Moundridge.

Tim is a graduate of the Associated Mennonite Biblical Seminaries in Elkhart, Indiana. He and his wife, Paula, have a teenage daughter, Kristin.

About the Illustrator

Paula Diller Lehman services as co-pastor of Faith Mennonite Church in Minneapolis, Minnesota, with her husband, Tim. Paula leads women's wilderness trips for Wilderness Wind.

A native of Ohio, Paula attended college in Michigan and Ohio. She is a graduate of the Associated Mennonite Biblical Seminaries in Elkhart, Indiana.

Paula directed youth ministry programs, including service programs, for the General Conference Mennonite Church during the nine years she and her family lived in central Kansas.

Paula and her husband have a teenage daughter, Kristin.